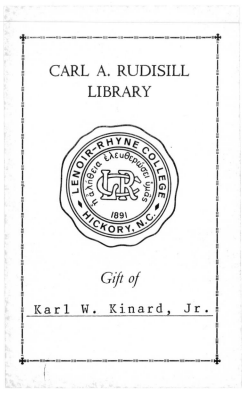

Opera

Opera

CAROLE ROSEN

Blandford Press
Poole · Dorset

First published in the U.K. 1983 by Blandford
Press, Link House, West Street, Poole,
Dorset, BH15 1LL.

Copyright © 1983 Carole Rosen

Distributed in the United States by
Sterling Publishing Co., Inc.,
2 Park Avenue, New York, N.Y. 10016.

British Library Cataloguing in Publication Data

Rosen, Carole
  Opera.
  1. Opera
  I. Title
  782.1   ML1700

ISBN 0 7137 1194 9

Typeset by August Filmsetting, Warrington, Cheshire.

Printed by Shenval Marketing Ltd.

Contents

Picture Credits

The photographs and illustrations were supplied and/or reproduced by kind permission of the following:

Introduction

When I told an architect friend that I was writing a brief book on opera, he asked if it would tell him 'what he was missing'. The feeling that he was missing something was a step in the right direction, but the fact that he had lived in England for 45 years without setting foot in the theatre for an opera performance was a reflection on the small part that opera plays in the lives of the majority of intelligent and otherwise culturally aware people in Britain.

Handel and the popularity of *Messiah* are usually blamed for the relative absence of English interest in opera. Its basic appeal is to the heart, not the head; unlike the Italians, the British find the unabashed outpouring of emotion and passionate melody in *La Bohème* or *Tosca* a little embarrassing in its effusiveness. Unlike the Italians, the Germans and even the French, the British have no native operatic tradition of long standing and thus opera has remained a largely suspect foreign import, indulged in by the rich, somehow tainted with decadent opulence and condemned by intellectuals on the old premise that 'anything too silly to be said, could be sung'.

Opera is not really like that at all. Half of its origins is aristocratic, but the other vital half is firmly rooted in the songs, stories and dances of popular entertainment through the centuries from Monteverdi's *Orfeo* to Bernstein's *West Side Story*. In today's world, effortless entertaiment is available at the pressing of a button. It may be the chance hearing of Carmen's 'Habanera' on the car radio that captivates the innocent ear and leads its owner first to the record shop and then to the theatre. Records are an excellent preparation for the vocal beauty and orchestral splen-

7

dour, but the glamour, warmth and excitement of opera can only be fully enjoyed at a live performance.

The object of this book is to provide the background to opera for the relative newcomer who has tried a few of the dishes, likes the taste and now wants to find out more about the cooking. As I am a professional singer, my stance is decidedly partisan, but I am fully aware of the difficulties of bringing opera out of the museum and into the market place. Like love, opera is for everyone to enjoy. I hope this book may urge my architect friend and many like him into the theatre to find out for themselves what they are missing. Opera is essentially live art and it can only continue to grow if it has a growing, live audience.

I

The beginnings of opera — the Classical Age

Italy

The ancestors of opera were to a great extent religious in nature. Greek drama grew out of Dionysian religious ceremonies and in the Middle Ages liturgical dramas developed from the practice of priests acting out various episodes in the life of Christ, particularly the Nativity, Crucifixion and Resurrection. Costumes, actions and scenery, together with hymn tunes or popular melodies and the congregation joining in as a chorus, established the basic ingredients of opera. Gradually the performances moved outside the church and developed into more elaborate mystery plays organised by professional trade guilds with instrumental music and songs. In Italy they were known as *Sacre Rappresentazioni* (sacred performances) and were entirely sung.

The first known secular play with music was *Le Jeu de Robin et de Marion* (The Play of Robin and Marion) with music by Adam de la Halle, performed at the court of the King of Naples in about 1283. One of the features of Renaissance Italy in the fifteenth and sixteenth centuries was secular drama, with elaborate costumes and scenery, in which music for voices and instruments was used for the interludes (*intermedii*) between the acts of the play. Often the music was in the form of five- or six-part madrigals and a number of madrigal comedies were also written. The most famous of these was *L'Amfiparnasso* (The Lower Slopes of Parnassus, 1597) by Orazio Vecchi.

It is convenient to date opera as we understand the term today from 1597 and the first performance in Florence of *Dafne*, a drama

9

based on the Greek legend of the god Apollo and the nymph Daphne, written by the poet Ottavio Rinuccini and set to music by Jacopo Peri (1561–1633). Unfortunately most of this music has been lost, but their next collaboration, *Euridice*, written for the wedding celebrations of Henry IV of France and Marie de' Medici in 1600 has survived, together with a second setting of the text by Giulio Caccini (*c.* 1545–1618), father of the first operatic soprano to become a popular prima donna.

Rinuccini, Peri and Caccini were members of the Florentine Camerata, a group of scholars, poets, musicians and aristocratic amateurs who met at the house of their wealthy patron Count Bardi (1534–1612). Like all artists of the Renaissance movement, they looked to the classical worlds of ancient Greece and Rome for their inspiration. Vincenzo Galilei (*c.* 1520–91), father of the famous astronomer, had published *Dialogue about Ancient and Modern Music* (*c.* 1581) from which the other composers of the Camerata evolved their 'new music'. As a reaction against polyphonic madrigals, in which a number of voices sing different melodies at the same time, they concentrated on a succession of solo voices accompanied by a small group of stringed instruments, and believed that they were reviving the practice of the ancient Greeks. It is extremely difficult to be sure how Greek dramas were originally performed; Peri came to the conclusion that it was half way between ordinary speech and actual melodic singing. He evolved the *stile rappresentativo* (theatre style) which became the distinctive mark of the Florentine opera; a melodic line which followed the natural rhythms, accents and inflections of the text and expressed the emotions of the character in each dramatic situation. As in Greek plays, dramatic incidents like the death of Euridice happened off-stage and were then described in sung narrative (recitative). A chorus of ten or twelve singers who both sang and danced was used to comment on the action.

Rather like Columbus, who set off for the East Indies and accidentally discovered America, the Florentine Camerata, thinking they were reviving authentic Greek drama, stumbled on a totally new artistic combination of words, music and action and invented opera. It was left to a composer of genius, Claudio Monteverdi (1567–1643), to show the full potential of their discovery. His first opera, *Orfeo* was performed in Mantua in 1607. Already a composer of considerable reputation in madrigals and sacred music, he was able to combine the harmonic interest of polyphony with the new monodic style of the Florentines. He used a large orchestra and a wide variety of instruments to heighten the dramatic action and the emotions of the singers. The following year he composed *Arianna* for the wedding of his patron's son, Francesco Gonzago, to Margherita of Savoy before 6,000 guests. The only fragment to survive is the famous lament, opera's first popular 'hit', which owes much of its poignancy to the untimely death of Monteverdi's own wife.

Claudio Monteverdi (1567–1643)

The new form of entertainment quickly spread to other cities in Tuscany and Lombardy, as well as to Rome and Naples. Comic interludes were first introduced into stories of classical heroes and heroines, then comic opera developed as a separate form with romantic plots interspersed with scenes featuring stock *commedia dell'arte* characters or ordinary working people. *Chi soffre, speri* (Who suffers may hope) with music by Vergilio Mazzocchi and words by Giulio Rospigliosi, the future Pope Clement IX, was first performed in Rome (1637) and featured a special musical style for realistic comic dialogue: quick moving, sharply accentuated, semi-musical speech, accompanied by sustained chords, which developed into the distinctive *recitativo secco* of later Italian opera.

All these operas were lavish events which could only be organised by wealthy princes for special festivities and for which temporary theatres would be built. In 1637 the first permanent public opera house was opened in Venice. Instead of a refined court spectacle, opera became a popular entertainment. By the end of the seventeenth century, 388 operas had been produced in Venice and the city was supporting six regular opera companies.

When he was over 70, Monteverdi wrote his last two great works for public theatres in Venice: *Il Ritorno d'Ulisse in Patria* (The Return of Ulysses, 1641) and *L'Incoronazione di Poppea* (The Coronation of Poppea, 1642). Monteverdi was the first to introduce ensemble singing into opera, duets, trios etc., and to develop the recitative style into an extended expression of emotion in beautiful vocal melody which became known as an aria.

After his death, operatic leadership was shared by his pupil Francesco Cavalli (1602–76), two of whose works, *L'Ormindo* (1644) and *La Calisto* (1651), have been successfully revived in recent years, and Pietro Antonio Cesti (1623–69). Cavalli was the first composer to use the term 'opera' to describe his work, referring to his first dramatico-musical work in 1639 as an *opera*

Monteverdi's opera The Coronation of Poppea *produced by the English National Opera (1971)*

scenica and not as a *dramma per musica*, the previously accepted name. Cesti, a Franciscan monk with an excellent tenor voice became chief composer at the Austrian Court and composed *Il Pomo d'Oro* (The Golden Apple) for the wedding of Emperor Leopold I to the Infanta Margherita of Spain in 1666.

Venice, a city of great wealth and a centre of international trade attracted many foreign visitors; among them was the diarist John Evelyn, who described the opera there as 'one of the most magnificent and expensive diversions the wit of man can invent'. Once it became commercialised, it became standardised; the chorus disappeared and the orchestra, now based on a small string group dominated by violins instead of the softer-toned viols, was placed at the front of the stage. Trumpets and drums were added for martial music and flutes or recorders for romantic scenes. Venetian audiences wanted stories of human beings in love, not tales of ancient mythology expressed in beautiful poetry.

Most of the opera houses were primitive and dirty buildings with wooden seats. The management lavished their money on elaborate stage scenery, cloud machines, transformation effects and the large fees demanded by popular singers. For the sake of virtuoso soloists, elaborate arias which bore no relation to the dramatic story but gave ample scope for showy displays of vocal agility and decoration known as *coloratura*, were interpolated in the score. The most famous soprano was Adriana Basile for whose services kings competed; when she returned to Naples, the city of her birth, she was greeted by the entire population. John Milton dedicated three Latin poems to her daughter Leonora Baroni when he heard her sing in Rome. Female sopranos and contraltos were challenged in popularity by the *castrati*, artificially preserved male sopranos and altos who combined the female vocal range with the power of men's lungs. Cultivated in cathedral choirs, they were originally used to circumvent the papal ban against women appearing on stage, but their sexless tones soon became fashionable in male roles as well.

By the end of the seventeenth century supremacy in the operatic field had passed to Naples, the largest city in Italy, whose opulent court encouraged music in every way. The Neapolitan composers tried to restore opera to the ideals of its original founders by reforming the type of texts that were set to music. Instead of an illogical assortment of songs, comic turns and rude jokes, operatic texts became once again classical stories of noble characters and high moral principles with clearly defined plots influenced by the great French dramatist Racine. The most highly regarded operatic dramatist of the eighteenth century was Pietro Metastasio (1698–1782), court poet at Vienna, whose texts were given over 1,000 musical settings by composers throughout Europe. His plays were elegant rather than powerful, stocked with conventional stereotypes instead of real, convincing people. His verse form of two contrasting quatrains was ideal for the *da capo* aria in three parts, beginning with a statement, followed by a middle section in contrasting mood and concluding with a repetition of the statement in which the vocal melody is ornamented by the singer to display his or her skill.

The leader of the Neapolitan school was Alessandro Scarlatti (1660–1725) who first found fame in Rome as composer and conductor to ex-Queen Christina of Sweden. He standardised the operatic overture by giving it three definite sections, and fully developed the *da capo* aria so that it could be used equally well to express joy or despair, rage or sorrow. He also introduced popular songs and dance rhythms for lighter arias which increased the popularity of his operas. He developed a new dimension for recitative by adding a stringed accompaniment, making it a far more emotional vehicle for relating dramatic off-stage happenings. His final invention was the 'ensemble of perplexity' in which four or more characters express their differing reactions to the same situation simultaneously, in a manner not possible in a spoken play.

Unfortunately the emphasis on the *da capo* aria became a straightjacket for Italian *opera seria* (serious opera). Dialogue was neglected and singers demanded these arias in every scene and on every entry to display their vocal virtuosity regardless of the plot and dramatic relevance. By the middle of the eighteenth century, all Europe was dominated by operas that were merely a succession of beautiful melodies and indulgent vocal fireworks.

France

France was the one European country which managed to develop an operatic tradition of its own, recognisably independent from the Italian model. Italian opera failed to flourish on French soil despite the all-pervading influence of Cardinal Mazarin, the Chief Minister, who brought Francesco Cavalli from Venice to produce his opera *Serse* for the wedding festivities of Louis XIV and Maria Teresa of Spain in 1660. The nobles of the French court were more impressed by Giacomo Torelli's (1608–78) elaborate scenery and stage machinery than the singers, and particularly disliked hearing a male soprano, a Servite priest, in the role of Queen Amestris. Two years later Cavalli's *Ercole amante* (Hercules in love), commissioned to celebrate the Peace of the Pyrenees, met with more success as it included many ballet scenes with music by another Italian, known in his adopted country as Jean-Baptiste Lully (1632–87).

Florentine by birth, Lully had been brought to the French court at the age of 14 and his skill as a violinist and talent as a dancer quickly made him a favourite companion of the young king who was passionately fond of ballet. Lully collaborated with the great French dramatist Molière to create a new art form, *comédie-ballet*, a highly stylised combination of singing, dancing, comedy and spectacle, the best known example being *Le Bourgeois Gentilhomme* (1670), which nearly two-and-a-half centuries later was to inspire Richard Strauss's opera *Ariadne auf Naxos* (Stuttgart, 1912).

In 1669, Louis XIV granted a patent to the composer Robert Cambert (*c.* 1628–77) and his librettist Pierre Perrin to build an opera house for public performances before a paying public. The Académie Royale de Musique opened with *Pomone* in 1671. Lully, who had previously maintained that opera in French was doomed to failure, ousted his two rivals in 1672 and gained control of the Académie together with the monopoly from Louis XIV over all operatic performances in France.

In partnership with the dramatic poet Philippe Quinault (1635–88), he composed *Cadmus et Hermione*, a *tragédie en musique*, staged in 1673. This set the pattern for the works he produced annually with resounding success until his death in 1687. Every opera opened with a prologue of gods and goddesses eulogising Louis XIV. As with the Venetian operas, the subjects were ancient legends and Renaissance epics, but Lully and Quinault ensured that they remained true to the spirit of the Classical age, as stories of love and heroism without any comment on contemporary characters or events. The King's love of ballet was requited by the frequent insertion of incidental ballet scenes. Ballet remained an

Ballet: integral part of French opera for 200 years. In 1861 Wagner had to revise *Tannhaüser* and turn the first scene into a great ballet-pantomime for its première at the Paris Opéra.

One of Lully's greatest achievements was the creation of a musical recitative style specially suited to the French language; he modelled this on the declamation used in the great tragedies of Racine and Corneille by the Comédie Française. The text had to be of the highest standard before he started composing and he always fitted the music to the words. His vocal 'airs' were very different from the arias of Italian opera, being shorter, simpler and demanding far less agility and vocal brilliance. His three master-pieces, *Alceste* (1674), *Thésée* (1675) and *Armide* (1686) remained in the repertoire of the Paris Opéra for almost 100 years. They contain many scenes which have nothing to do with furthering the action but exist solely to give pleasure to the ear and eye: idyllic pastorals, masques, gala scenes, fantastical sylphs, nymphs and satyrs which became standard elements in future operatic plots. They were the excuse not only for dances and choruses but instrumental numbers as well.

The secret of Lully's success lay in his perfectionism and his versatility. He supervised the stage settings and costumes, and acted as producer and choreographer as well as being in charge of the musical preparation. He worked tirelessly with singers and dancers until every detail was perfect. The King ordered that all works performed at the Académie should be published at state expense, thus Lully's operas have been preserved.

His orchestral forces were much larger than those of the Venetians: flutes, oboes, bassoons, trumpets, timpani and harpsi-chord were added to the excellent string section, the *Vingt-Quatre Violins du Roi* of the court orchestra. Lully developed the so-called 'French overture' in two movements, the first slow and majestic with dotted rhythms followed by a quicker more lively section, which became one of the most influential musical forms of the late baroque period and was frequently used by both Bach and Handel. Lully used a large wooden wand to conduct his orchestra and his premature death was caused by gangrene after accidentally striking his foot with it.

French opera had to wait for nearly half a century for a fitting follower to Lully when Jean-Philippe Rameau (1683–1764) wrote his first work for the stage, *Hippolyte et Aricie* (1733). He had

16

Original title page of Lully's opera Alceste *published in 1674*

already made his reputation as a composer of church music and the author of a treatise on harmony which had far-reaching effects. His operas were dedicated to the glory of Louis XV in the same way that Lully's had extolled his royal great-grandfather. They accepted the conventions of a bygone age but musically they were criticised for being too noisy and in advance of their time. He developed the dramatic function of the chorus as well as the complexity of the music which it had to sing. Above all he is distinguished for the instrumental music of his operas, particularly his descriptive writing conveying the beauty of the landscape, the terror of storms, earthquakes and off-stage battles, which fore-shadows the Romantic movement and the programme music of Berlioz. Among his greatest operas are *Castor et Pollux* (1737), *Zorastre* (1749) and *Les Indes Galantes* (1735), which had a sumptuous revival at the Paris Opéra in 1952 followed by more than 200 performances in the next 10 years.

England

The origins of opera in England lay in the masque, a combination of spoken dialogue, music and dance devised as a royal diversion for the courts of Elizabeth I, James I and Charles I. The splendour of these productions, which were influenced by Italian opera and copied the recitative style of singing, can be gauged from drawings by Inigo Jones preserved at Chatsworth House in Derbyshire. One of the best known masques was *Comus* performed at Ludlow Castle in 1634 with words by Milton and music, unfortunately mostly now lost, by Henry Lawes (1596–1662).

England nearly had the first public opera house to be built outside Italy, for in 1639, Sir William Davenant, then Poet Laureate and reputed to be the bastard son of Shakespeare, was licensed by Charles I to open a theatre for the public performance of plays, concerts and operas. The Civil War put an end to his plans as Cromwell and the Puritans considered the theatre a place of immorality. Instead, in 1656, Davenant staged the first of three English operas, *The Siege of Rhodes*, on a small stage at Rutland House in Charterhouse Yard, London, calling the five acts 'entries' and describing the work as 'A Representation by the Art of Prospective in Scenes and the Story sung in Recitative Musick'. The music was by Henry Lawes and Matthew Locke.

The Restoration of Charles II was a double set-back to English opera: once the ban on spoken drama was removed the English indulged their preference for plays with incidental music, and Charles, returning from exile with a preference for French composers, appointed Louis Grabu Master of the King's Music. He collaborated with the poet Dryden in an opera in the style of

Lully called *Albion and Albanius* (1685). Matthew Locke (*c.* 1630–77), who had established his reputation with the music for the masque *Cupid and Death* (1653), now wrote songs for Molière's *Psyche* and for popular new presentations of Shakespeare's *The Tempest* and *Macbeth* featuring witches who flew and sang. These were all performed at the resplendent new Dorset Garden Theatre designed by Sir Christopher Wren. Here for the first time the orchestra was placed in view of the audience at the front of the stage, instead of in a gallery over it, and was expanded to 24 strings and a harpsichord.

Henry Purcell (1659–95)

1st operatic masterpiece by English composer

The next attempt at an opera as we know it was the far more successful *Venus and Adonis* by John Blow (1649–1708), written for the private entertainment of the King (*c.* 1685). Venus was sung by his mistress Mary Davis and Cupid by their young daughter Lady Mary Tudor. It served as a model for Henry Purcell's *Dido and Aeneas* composed for the girls of Josias Priest's school in Chelsea in 1689. Although it lasts only an hour it is an operatic masterpiece of

enormous emotional range and dramatic power, still as effective
and moving today as it was 300 years ago. Trained as a choirboy in
the Chapel Royal, Purcell (1659–95) was organist at Westminster
Abbey and a prolific composer. In six years he wrote the music for
40 plays of which the most substantial were *Dioclesian* (1690), *King
Arthur* (1691) in collaboration with Dryden, *The Fairy Queen*
(1692) based on Shakespeare's *A Midsummer Night's Dream*, and
The Tempest (1695). Purcell and Dryden aimed to establish serious
opera in English, but popular taste did not support them and *Dido
and Aeneas* remained Purcell's only work sung throughout, being
without any spoken dialogue. With his untimely death at the age of
35, English opera died with him and Italian opera became
supreme.

   In 1711 George Frederick Handel (1685–1759) took London by
storm with *Rinaldo* sung entirely in Italian. During the next 30
years he composed 35 operas for the London stage. A disgruntled
law student from Halle (Saxony), Handel had followed his first
operatic success, *Almira*, in Hamburg in 1705 with five years in
Italy which shaped his operatic style. In 1719 George I commissioned Handel, who had been his director of court music in
Hanover, to set up an opera company under the patronage of the
newly formed Royal Academy of Music. Unfortunately, Lord
Burlington, principal financial sponsor of the venture also appointed Giovanni Bononcini (1670–1747) as associate composer. The
noble lords took sides and London had two Italian opera
companies vying with each other in the lavishness of their
productions and the vocal skills of their male and female sopranos.
The two prima donnas whom Handel engaged at an exorbitant fee
of £2,000 each a year, Francesca Cuzzoni and Faustina Bordoni,
ended by fighting on stage and pulling out handfulls of each
other's hair!

   The ridiculousness of these artistic squabbles was immortalised
in John Byrom's epigram:

> Some say that Signor Bononcini
> Compared to Handel's a mere ninny;
> Others aver, to him, that Handel
> Is scarcely fit to hold a candle.
> Strange! that such high dispute should be
> Twixt Tweedledum and Tweedledee.

Janet Baker in Dido and Aeneas *by Purcell at the Aldeburgh Festival (1962)*

Hogarth's depiction of a scene from The Beggar's Opera *by John Gay*

See
p. 116
in music
in Time

play example

An even more devastating parody, *The Beggar's Opera*, was performed at John Rich's theatre in Lincoln's Inn Fields in 1728. Dr. Pepusch's music ranged from popular songs to favourite melodies from Purcell and Handel; the author John Gay (1685–1732) pretended that the work had been written by a beggar to celebrate the wedding of two street singers, making fun of baroque opera commissioned to celebrate state occasions. Its hero was a highwayman surrounded by prostitutes, pimps and beggars; it satirised the corruption and immorality of political life and contemporary society. It was a phenomenal success and set the fashion for a hundred years of ballad operas, translated all over Europe, and the German *Singspiel*, comic opera with spoken dialogue and popular songs.

Undismayed by the failure of the Academy, Handel founded his own opera company for which his greatest works included *Orlando* (1733), *Ariodante* (1735) and *Alcina* (1735). Again he was opposed by a rival company, this time under the patronage of Frederick, Prince of Wales. Their greatest attraction was the castrato Carlo Broschi, called Farinelli, who, after his London success, moved across the English Channel to receive a portrait in diamonds from Louis XV in France and was then engaged to soothe the melancholy of Philip V of Spain with the same selection of arias repeated every night for ten years.

Handel ended with his health and his fortune ruined. He eventually turned to dramatic oratorio which, because it treated biblical subjects, could only be given in concert form. *Messiah* and *Israel in Egypt* present modern audiences with none of the problems of the operas. While enjoying the baroque magnificence of

Handel's music, a long string of glorious arias with very little dramatic or character development does not provide interesting action on the stage. According to the conventions of *opera seria* an aria presented the fixed mood of a character in a particular situation and not the ambiguity of real feelings. Handel excelled at expressing passion and heroic emotions, as in 'Lascia ch'io pianga' (O let me weep) from *Rinaldo*, 'Ombra mai fu' (Shade never was), the famous 'Largo' from *Serse* (1738), or Cleopatra's beautiful aria 'V'adoro, pupille' (Eyes that I adore) from *Giulio Cesare in Egitto* (1724).

One of the difficulties of modern productions of Handel's operas has been overcome in recent years by the number of male altos who, without undergoing physical emasculation, can sing castrati roles at their original pitch.

Handel's opera Alcina *with Joan Sutherland at Royal Opera House, Covent Garden (1961)*

Germany

The first German opera was a setting of Rinuccini's *Dafne* written by Heinrich Schütz, the great forerunner of J. S. Bach, for the marriage in 1627 of Princess Sophia Eleonora of Saxony to George Landgrave of Hesse at the castle of Torgau. The text by Martin Opitz has survived but none of the music, which was in the new Italian style. A more independent German work was *Das Geistliche Waldgedicht Seelewig* (The sacred woodland tale of Seelewig), by Siegmund Staden (1607–55), first performed in Nuremburg in 1644, which showed traces of the medieaval mystery plays. Grandiose operas on the Italian model flourished in the great royal courts of Vienna, Munich, Dresden and Hanover where they were given in Italian with a German text often provided so that the audience could understand what was happening on the stage. It was left to the smaller courts like Brunswick, Weissenfels, Leipzig and, above all, the city state of Hamburg, to encourage opera by German composers.

Hamburg's Goose Market Theatre which opened in 1678 with a Biblical comedy, *Adam und Eva*, was the first public opera house in Europe outside Italy. It reached its peak under Reinhard Keiser (1674–1739) who wrote 120 operas, sometimes at the rate of eight a year. His first popular success, *Störtebecker und Goedje Michel* (1701), dealt with the career of two local pirates recently executed and featured popular peasant characters, singing and speaking in the local dialect of Low German, and generous torrents of calf's blood flowing from pig's bladders which the singers concealed beneath their costumes. Despite the success of the great baroque composer George Philipp Telemann (1681–1767), who wrote 20 operas for the Hamburg stage, German opera was finally vanquished by the Neapolitans and in 1738 the Goose Market Theatre was closed and eventually demolished.

Frederick the Great of Prussia compared German singing to the neighing of horses; when an opera house was finally built in Berlin in 1740 under the directorship of an Italianised German, Karl Heinrich Grau (1704–59), the Italian fashion prevailed. The musical director of the Dresden Opera from 1731 to 1763 was Johann Adolph Hasse (1699–1783), trained in Naples and married to the famous soprano Faustina Bordoni. He was more Italian than the Italians who called him *Il caro sassone* (the beloved Saxon); his

50 operas, mostly to libretti of Metastasio, epitomise *opera seria* which had become the unrivalled form of courtly musical entertainment throughout Europe. He travelled frequently to present his works in Warsaw, London, Prague and Vienna.

In Vienna the tradition had been established at the court of Leopold I under Antonio Draghi (1635–1700), followed by Antonio Caldara (1670–1736) and Johann Joseph Fux (1660–1741), one of whose grandest productions was *Costanza e Fortezza* (Constancy and Fortitude) staged in a specially built auditorium in Prague for the coronation of Charles VI in 1723.

By the middle of the eighteenth century certain composers were beginning to rebel against the rigid conventions of *opera seria* in which music had to take second place to a complicated and highly stylised libretto. Tommaso Traetta (1727–79) at the court at Parma and Niccolò Jommelli (1714–74) at Stuttgart both aimed for a greater simplicity and fluidity in their operas, breaking down the old design where elaborate formal arias halted the dramatic action. They followed the principles established by Francesco Algarotti in his *Essay on the Opera* (1755); French influence caused them to place greater emphasis on the contribution of both ballet and chorus, while German influence resulted in a more imaginative use of the orchestra and a wider range of instruments.

The real honour for operatic reform is due to a German composer of Bohemian origin, Christoph Willibald Gluck (1714–87). He had enjoyed a varied career as writer of conventional operas in Italy and Vienna before his first great masterpiece *Orfeo ed Euridice* was performed in 1762 at the court of Maria Theresa. His librettist was an Italian, Ranieri Calzabigi (1714–95); they strove to return to the principles of music drama evolved by the Florentine Camerata 150 years before. There are only three characters in the opera: Orfeo, originally sung by a male alto, Euridice and Amor; instead of florid display, the vocal lines are of great simplicity and deep emotional feeling. The story is presented in a series of tableaux, the effect of which depends greatly on ballet and chorus. Gluck rewrote the work for performance in Paris in 1774 with a tenor in the title role. In 1859 Berlioz combined the two versions for the great contralto Pauline Viardot-Garcia. It remains the earliest work to hold a regular place in the modern operatic repertoire, a star vehicle for contraltos, culminating in 'Che faro', Orfeo's despairing anguish at the loss of Euridice.

Orfeo played by Janet Baker in Glyndebourne's production of Orfeo ed Euridice
by Gluck (1982)

Calzabigi and Gluck prefaced their next opera *Alceste* (1767) with a clear statement of their reforming intentions: 'to purify music from all the abuses which have crept into Italian opera through the vanity of the singers and the excessive compliance of the composers and have made the most splendid and beautiful of all arts the most ridiculous and boring'. Their third opera *Paride ed Elena* (Paris and Helen, 1770) is so stripped of extraneous action as to be almost static and concentrates on the changing emotional states of its hero and heroine.

Gluck's new operas found far greater favour in Paris than in Vienna, particularly *Iphigénie en Aulide*, performed under the patronage of Marie Antoinette in 1774. A rival faction was formed to champion the Italian composer Niccolò Piccinni (1728–1800) and they were both asked to compose music for the same libretto. Gluck's last triumph was *Iphigénie en Tauride* (1779), a work which comes as close as possible to being a modern revival of the spirit of Greek tragedy.

Gluck's favourite pupil, Antonio Salieri (1750–1825), is remembered today as the man accused of having poisoned Mozart. In Italy Gluck's style was spread by Simone Mayr (1763–1845), followed by Saverio Mercadante (1795–1870). His successors in France were: Étienne Méhul (1763–1817) whose main work *Joseph* (1807) is distinguished by an absence of female characters; Gasparo Spontini (1774–1851) who enjoyed his greatest operatic triumph with *La Vestale* (The Vestal Virgin, 1807); and Luigi Cherubini (1760–1842) whose tragedy *Médée* (1797), like the previous work, was revived in the 1950s for Maria Callas.

Mozart

Wolfang Amadeus Mozart's (1756–91) sublime genius comes as a fitting climax to the Classical Age of the eighteenth century and the supremacy of Italian opera, but it also forms a bridge to the development of German Romantic opera in the nineteenth century. Mozart treated characters in opera, for the first time, as real people with whom an audience could identify and whose personalities developed during the course of the stage action, instead of as stock types, either heroic or comic, presented as generalisations. They have a timeless, universal appeal; a late twentieth-century audience can appreciate the predicament of

Donna Anna in *Don Giovanni* or the Countess in *Le Nozze di Figaro* (The Marriage of Figaro) without any knowledge of the operatic conventions of 200 years ago. Mozart was blessed with a superb dramatic sense; his plots are consistent and the action makes dramatic as well as psychological sense. Above all, it is the music which makes his operas such easily accessible masterpieces: the melodies of his arias, his use of recitative as natural sounding conversation and his mastery of symphonic composition, deploying the orchestra and the tone colours of various instruments like the clarinet, 'cello or trombone to highlight a particular emotion or underline a dramatic effect.

He wrote his first opera at the age of eight and amongst his early successes was *Bastien und Bastienne*, performed in Vienna at the private theatre of the hypnotist Franz Mesmer (1768). In 1781 he was commissioned to write *Idomeneo* for the Munich Court Theatre and it is in many ways the finest *opera seria* of the late eighteenth century. In the last year of his life, when his creative powers and experience had moved far beyond the artificialities of this archaic operatic vehicle, he hurriedly composed *La Clemenza di Tito* (The Clemency of Titus) in 18 days for the coronation of Leopold II in Prague.

Mozart's artistic vitality was far better suited to the comic muse, demonstrated in *Die Entführung aus dem Serail* (The Abduction from the Seraglio) written in 1782 for the German National Singspiel Theatre founded by Leopold II in Vienna. It is an ebullient mixture of Italian comic opera (*opera buffa*), German dialogue and an English plot with fashionable oriental musical trimmings. The opera's heroine is called Constanze, after Mozart's wife, but its popular success brought disappointingly little financial reward to the newly married couple.

Mozart now found his ideal librettist in Lorenzo da Ponte (1749–1838), a reprobate adventurer, Jewish convert and failed priest, to whom he suggested Beaumarchais' comedy *Le Mariage de Figaro*. The play was banned in Vienna as politically inflammatory, but once set to music Figaro became an acceptable comic servant, a descendant of *commedia dell'arte*'s Scapino, instead of a potential revolutionary challenging the authority of his despotic master, Count Almaviva. Mozart's music makes *Le Nozze di Figaro* a scintillating masterpiece in which each character comes to life as a sharply delineated real person in an effervescent atmosphere of

Wolfgang Amadeus Mozart (1756–91)

Kiri te Kanawa as the Countess and Geraint Evans as Figaro in Mozart's Le Nozze di Figaro *at Covent Garden (1971)*

rococo elegance and charm. Moments of seriousness throw the comic situations into greater relief. Above all it is Mozart's use of ensembles (especially the finales of Acts II and IV) as compositions for voices and orchestra, developed in the same way as a symphony, which show his masterly organisation of musical form.

Figaro enjoyed greater success in Prague than in Vienna and resulted in a commission for a new work there, *Don Giovanni* (or *The Libertine Punished*). Da Ponte described it as a comedy. Later interpreters have looked for a hero who set himself above social conventions, like Byron's Don Juan, rather than the version known to Mozart's contemporaries, a puppet-like figure whose amorous adventures end in disaster. This explains the final sextet in front of the curtain, where those he has duped point the moral of the notorious blasphemer and seducer receiving his punishment in hell.

Mozart and da Ponte's third collaboration, *Così fan tutte* (Women are all alike, 1790), is very much a Viennese period piece which can only be interpreted as a delightful comment on the fickleness of young ladies in love and the cynicism of the old bachelor who puts their affections to the test.

Scene from original production of Die Zauberflöte *by Mozart in Vienna in 1791*

Mozart's last opera *Die Zauberflöte* (The Magic Flute, 1791) was composed to a story by his old friend Emanuel Schikaneder who needed a spectacular 'magic' opera to save his Theatre auf der Wieden. They were both committed Freemasons, a force of considerable political importance in eighteenth-century Europe, and so decided to represent the conflict between the power of evil, the Queen of the Night, and the exponent of moral duties and virtues, Sarastro, using Masonic symbolism. Mozart used an enormous variety of musical styles: the elaborate coloratura of opera seria for the Queen of the Night, German folk song for Papageno with his pan-pipes, a Gluck-like choral refrain for the priests, musical drama for the heroine Pamina and the sexless quality of boys' voices for the magic element of the three genii. Mozart welded these diverse elements into a unique whole, imbued with a German spirit of mysticism and morality which was to lead the way to the music drama of Wagner.

play example from magic Flute

2

The nineteenth century –
Romantic opera

German Romantic opera

Ludwig van Beethoven (1770–1827) was a unique colossus bestriding the Classical eighteenth century and the Romantic movement of the nineteenth century. His one opera, *Fidelio*, is imbued with the spirit of humanitarian idealism, the main-spring of the French Revolution, and the triumph of individual heroism against tyranny and political oppression. He had great difficulty in finding a libretto which satisfied his high moral and dramatic standards and never managed to fulfil his life-long ambition of setting Goethe's *Faust* to music. Instead his enthusiasm was fired by Pierre Gaveaux's opera *Léonore, ou l'Amour conjugal* (Leonora or Conjugal Love, 1798) which the French librettist Jean Nicholas Bouilly based on an episode during the Reign of Terror. It was typical of the popular 'rescue operas' of the time. Beethoven's German version, *Fidelio*, produced in 1805 only played for three nights in Vienna as the city had just been occupied by Napoleon's troops, who formed the bulk of the audience. Both libretto and music were extensively revised and finally performed with great success in 1814. Although Leonora and Florestan are portrayed as real people, Beethoven's intellectual idealism and transcendent musical genius translate the opera from the realm of individual human emotions to create an overwhelming tribute to heroism and the triumphant virtue of mankind.

In music, as in literature and painting, the individual now reigned supreme, free to assert his freedom from political oppression, from conventional society and from the restraints of

Gwyneth Jones as Fidelio in Covent Garden production (1970) of Beethoven's only opera

old-fashioned artistic disciplines. In the realm of the imagination, the fantastic, the mysterious and the macabre were important elements in all romantic art, offering an escape from the horrors of the French Revolution and the Napoleonic Wars. The German poet, painter and composer E. T. A. Hoffmann (1776–1822), whom Offenbach was later to immortalise, started the fashion of opera as the new world of magic and fairy tale. In 1813 he wrote, 'I believe romantic opera is the only genuine opera, for music belongs in the realm of romanticism alone', and exemplified his ideas in *Undine*, produced in 1816 in Berlin.

Carl Maria von Weber (1786–1826) set the seal on the success of German romantic opera with *Der Freischütz* (The Marksman, Berlin 1821), based on the old folk legend of the wild huntsman and the magic bullets cast in the haunted glen. Weber's precocious musical talents had been fostered in his father's group of strolling players and his first opera was professionally produced when he was 13. Determined to produce a distinctively German style of opera, he had a long and bitter struggle against the rivalry and intrigue of Italian companies led by Francesco Morlacchi (1784–1841) in Dresden and Spontini in Berlin. *Der Freischütz* was hailed as a triumph and swept through Germany and Europe and even reached New York in 1825. Its enormous popular success was

Wolf's Glen scene from nineteenth-century production of Weber's Der Freischütz *at Covent Garden*

due to its blend of rustic simplicity, including village dances and choruses which have become part of German folk music, contrasted with the appealing melodies of its arias; it has a straightforward and exciting story in which the hero and heroine, an ordinary boy and girl, struggle against the powers of evil and the supernatural, portrayed by Weber with superb use of orchestral colouring.

Euryanthe, commissioned for the Kärntnertor Theatre in Vienna in 1823, was based on a French story of the Age of Chivalry; Weber replaced spoken dialogue, inherited from the *Singspiel* tradition, with continuous music including passages of recitative. The power of his music was unable to overcome the muddled text but the opera exerted a strong influence on Wagner's early works. Weber's last opera, *Oberon*, was commissioned by Charles Kemble for Covent Garden; unfortunately he was again hampered by a diffuse plot (by James Robinson Planché (1796–1880) who was famous for his pantomimes) which was sent to him act by act, and he decided to return to spoken dialogue. He was already mortally ill by the time he arrived in London and died shortly after conducting the traumatic première in 1826.

Thanks to Weber, German romantic opera was now triumphant and the last remaining Italian opera company was dismissed from Dresden in 1832. Heinrich Marschner (1795–1861), who had been assistant conductor to Weber at the court theatre there, proved to be one of his most successful disciples. His operas include a setting of *Der Vampyr* (The Vampire, attributed to Byron) and *Hans Heiling*, which is still performed in Germany.

Comic romantic opera has retained great popularity in German provincial opera houses, particularly the works of Albert Lortzing (1801–51): *Zar und Zimmermann* (Tsar and Carpenter, Leipzig 1837), based on the tale of Peter the Great's stay in disguise in Holland, *Der Wildschutz* (The Poacher, 1842) and *Der Waffenschmied* (The Armourer, Vienna 1846). Outside Germany the best known work in this genre is *Martha* (Vienna, 1847), by Friedrich von Flotow (1812–83), which is famous for its tenor aria 'M'appari', a favourite of Caruso's, and its use of Tom Moore's Irish melody, 'The Last Rose of Summer'. A much more robust comic opera is Otto Nicolai's (1810–49) version of Shakespeare's *The Merry Wives of Windsor* which was first performed in Berlin in 1849.

French grand opera

At the beginning of the nineteenth century Paris became the musical capital of Europe. The operatic themes of the period reflected the troubled political situation following the French Revolution; in fact one opera sparked off the Belgian Revolution of 1830. Daniel Auber's (1782–1871) *La Muette de Portici* (The Dumb Girl of Portici, Paris 1828), which dealt with the uprising of the Neapolitans against the Spanish in 1647, so inflamed the Belgians when it was performed in Brussels that they revolted against the Dutch and won their independence as a separate state. The libretto was by Eugène Scribe (1791–1861) who became the most sought after literary architect of French grand opera. This development expanded the style of Lully and Rameau to grandiose proportions. The stories were melodramatic historical epics, lavishly staged, with extensive ballets, crowd scenes and choruses interspersing brilliant arias designed to display the vocal prowess of the day's popular operatic stars. Typical of the style was *La Juive* (The Jewess), first performed in Paris in 1835, by Fromental

Halévy (1799–1862). His most famous pupil at the Paris Conservatoire was Bizet who married his daughter.

The foremost exponent of French grand opera was a German, Jakob Beer, who found fame in Paris as Giacomo Meyerbeer (1791–1864). Scribe provided the libretti for many of his Paris successes, the first of which was *Robert le Diable* (Robert the Devil) in 1831 and featured a spectacular ballet for the ghosts of nuns who had died in carnal sin. It was the opera in which the famous Swedish soprano Jenny Lind (1820–87) made her debut at Covent Garden. His next opera, *Les Huguenots* (1836) was based on the St Bartholemew's day massacre of 1572; *Le Prophète* (1849) also had a religious theme, the rising of the Münster Anabaptists under John of Leyden. For the first time the leading role in an opera was given to an older woman when Pauline Viardot-Garcia sang Fidès and created the prototype heroic mother and the fashion for dramatic contralto roles (e.g. Verdi's Azucena). His last opera and perhaps his best, *L'Africaine* (The African Maid), was not performed until after his death in 1865.

L'Africaine is occasionally revived today as a vehicle for a great black soprano (for example, Grace Bumbry in Covent Garden's 1981 production), but in general Meyerbeer's works, which were the staple of the world's opera houses for more than 50 years, are now dismissed as ludicrously outdated and overblown. This is in ironic contrast to the operas of Hector Berlioz (1803–69) which aroused enormous controversy and were ruled out as commercially and artistically impossible by most of his contemporaries. He is now recognised as perhaps the greatest French operatic composer of the nineteenth century and sumptuous productions of *Les Troyens* (The Trojans) are welcomed as events of great prestige.

Berlioz was the epitome of the romantic artist and his *Memoirs* give a highly coloured account of his adventures in life and love and his constant struggle for recognition against professional prejudice and jealousy. His most influential book was *Treatise on Modern Instrumentation and Orchestration* (1844) which showed the enormous development of orchestral instruments, particularly woodwind and brass, since Beethoven's time. In composing his operatic works he made use of the great wealth of orchestral variety now at his disposal. *Benvenuto Cellini*, first performed in Paris in 1838, was the only one of his operas to be performed complete in France during his lifetime. *La Damnation de Faust*

Placido Domingo in L'Africaine *by Giacomo Meyerbeer at Covent Garden (1978)*

(1846) was written as a dramatic cantata but was later adapted for the operatic stage. His lightest work was *Béatrice et Bénédict*, based on Shakespeare's *Much Ado About Nothing*, an appropriate choice for Berlioz who had fallen in love with his future wife, the Irish Shakespearian actress Harriet Smithson, while she was playing Juliet. It was performed at Baden-Baden (1862) and Weimar (1863) as a result of Liszt's championship of Berlioz.

Hector Berlioz (1803–69)

Liszt's mistress, Princess Sayn-Wittgenstein, provided Berlioz with a dramatic outline for his long-standing ambition, to create an opera, eventually to be in two parts, from Books II and IV of Virgil's *Aeneid*. Part I was *La Prise de Troie* (The Capture of Troy) and Part II was *Les Troyens à Carthage* (The Trojans at Carthage). *Les Troyens* is undoubtedly the most important French opera of the nineteenth century and equal to Wagner's German *Ring* cycle,

The death of Dido from the first production of Berlioz's Les Troyens *in Paris in 1863*

although it has never achieved the same volume of public acclaim. It is an epic opera dealing with great legendary themes; individual passions are sacrificed to the cosmic plan which will eventually lead to the foundation of the Roman Empire. Berlioz's music is on a suitably epic scale, making no concessions to fashionable melodies of the time, but sweeping on in heroic vocal and orchestral grandeur. He eventually agreed to the second part alone being performed in Paris in 1863. He prefaced his own piano reduction of the vocal score with suggestions for cutting the work's length and staging costs, adding with tragic resignation, 'O my noble Cassandra [the heroine of Part I]! My heroic virgin, I shall never hear thee!' The complete work as he had conceived it was not performed until 1969 when both Scottish Opera and Covent Garden staged productions.

Opéra Comique

In addition to grand opera, Paris was the home of *opéra comique*, which had its origin in the entertainments played at the great annual fairs in Paris, and challenged the monopoly of the Opéra and the Comédie Française. It was given the seal of royal approval when a little work with words and music by Jean-Jacques Rousseau, *Le Devin du Village* (The Village Soothsayer), was performed at Fontainbleau before Louis XV in 1753. A feud developed between the protagonists of Italian opera, typified by Pergolesi's *La Serva Padrona* (The Maid as Mistress, 1752), and the new style of works in French with spoken dialogue instead of sung recitative. This was a pamphlet war known as the 'Querelle des Bouffons' (Quarrel of the Clowns).

Although many of the favourite subjects performed at the Opéra-Comique theatre had a rustic setting, often the plots were serious rather than comic, but still conformed to the mixture of singing and spoken dialogue. The first successful composer of *opéra comique* was a Belgian, André Ernest Grétry (1741–1813) whose best operas were *Richard Coeur de Lion* (Richard the Lion Heart, 1784) and *Zémire et Azore* (1771).

After the French Revolution the new middle class found *opéra comique* a far more approachable form of entertainment than grand opera. Amongst the most popular works were *La Dame Blanche* (The White Lady, 1825) by François Adrien Boïeldieu (1775–1834); *Fra Diavolo* (1830) by Auber; *Le Postillon de Longjumeau* (The Coachman of Longjumeau, 1836) by Adolphe Adam (1803–56) who is best known as composer of the ballet *Giselle*; and *Zampa or the Marble Betrothed* (1831), a gothic horror story by Ferdinand Hérold (1791–1833).

On the lighter side *opéra comique* developed into operetta (see Chapter 3); on the more serious side the French public expected, in contrast to the grandiose epics of Meyerbeer, less pretentious works which were unified in style and displayed distinctively French melodiousness and elegance. Both Ambroise Thomas (1811–96) and Charles Gounod (1818–93) achieved their initial successes at the Opéra-Comique, Thomas with *Mignon* (1866) based on Goethe's *Wilhelm Meister*, and Gounod with the original version of *Faust* (1859). Gounod later substituted sung recitative for the spoken dialogue and in this form *Faust* became the most frequently performed French opera, translated into 24 languages. His other successes included *Mireille* (1864) and *Roméo et Juliette* (1867).

The most significant work to be produced at the Opéra-Comique was *Carmen* by Georges Bizet (1838–75). Its tragic ending and the portrayal of a kind of passion and licentiousness not previously considered suitable for musical entertainment were unprecedented. Even so Bizet and his librettists, Henri Meilhac and Ludovic Halévy, considerably moderated the character of the amoral gipsy of Prosper Merimée's original novella (1845). *Carmen* was the first *verismo* (realistic) opera, dealing with the seamier

Mario and Adelina Patti in an 1864 production of Gounod's Faust *at Covent Garden*

Scene from English National Opera production of Massenet's Werther *with Janet Baker and John Brecknock (1977)*

passions of life rather than idealised emotions. The first-night audience was taken aback by the realism of Célestine Galli-Marié's 'Castilian licentiousness' and the opera was not given the wild critical and public acclaim for which Bizet had hoped. Nevertheless it was a success and when he died three months later it was receiving its twenty-third performance. The legend that he died of a broken heart at its failure is hard to scotch! The spoken dialogue was subsequently replaced by sung recitative and in this version Carmen has remained one of the most popular operas in the entire international repertoire.

Bizet's earlier works included a setting of Sir Walter Scott's *The Fair Maid of Perth* (*La Jolie Fille de Perth*, 1867) and *Les Pêcheurs de Perles* (The Pearl Fishers, 1863), which has an exotic setting in Ceylon. The 'mysterious East' became a favourite theme for French operatic composers; a notable example was *Lakmé* (1883) by Léo Delibes (1836–91) featuring a beautiful soprano from Brooklyn, Marie Van Zandt, as the hapless Hindu heroine. Camille Saint-Saëns (1835–1921) is also remembered for a sultry temptress, but one of Biblical origin in *Samson et Dalila*. Because the subject was considered unsuitable for stage presentation, Pauline Viardot-Garcia gave the second act in her garden, but when the opera was finally staged by Liszt in Weimar in 1877, she was too old to sing the role with conviction.

The most prolific and successful French operatic composer following Gounod was Jules Massenet (1842–1912) whose *Manon* (1884) makes an interesting comparison with Puccini's *Manon Lescaut* (Turin, 1893), a setting of Abbé Prévost's novel. Massenet's formula for success was to use a tragic and appealing leading lady presented in voluptuous melody and uncomplicated harmony. Following this recipe he produced one or two operas a year of which those of more lasting interest are *Hérodiade* (1881), *Werther* (1892) and *Thaïs* (1894). The most successful example of French operatic naturalism was written by one of Massenet's pupils, Gustave Charpentier (1860–1956); *Louise* (1900) is the touching story of a poor seamstress in Paris.

Wagner

No other composer aroused such passionate controversy or had a more far-reaching influence on the whole cultural and spiritual life of the nineteenth century than Richard Wagner (1813–83). Born in Leipzig, the stepson of an actor, he was a man of the theatre to his fingertips; his sisters were singers, his first wife, Minna Planer, was an actress and he learnt his craft as chorus-master and conductor in small provincial opera houses like Würzburg, Magdeburg and Riga. He knew that the public wanted excitement, drama, stirring spectacle and tragic love, all of which he provided in his earliest success *Rienzi*, based on the novel by Bulwer Lytton and composed in the grand opera style of Spontini and Meyerbeer. Meyerbeer's influence enabled it to be produced in Dresden in 1842 with two of Germany's best known singers, the tenor Tichatschek in the title role and the great soprano Schröder-Devrient in the boy's role of Adriano. Wagner envied Meyerbeer his unrivalled success and, according to one theory, his anti-Semitism sprang from jealousy of this one Jew.

Before his appointment as court conductor in Dresden, Wagner had been forced to flee with his wife to England to escape his creditors and then spent two years as an impoverished hack composer and journalist in Paris. Their near shipwreck on the Norwegian coast gave him the inspiration for his next opera *Der Fliegende Holländer* (The Flying Dutchman, Dresden 1843). This was the first truly symphonic opera in which the music grows continuously out of a few seminal themes, and the first of Wagner's operas expounding the theme of a sinful man redeemed by the love of a self-sacrificing woman.

The *Flying Dutchman*, *Tannhäuser* (Dresden, 1845), and *Lohengrin* (Weimar, 1850) form the climax of German romantic opera and are all based on legends of German mediaeval poetry. The evil couple, Ortrud and Telramund, in *Lohengrin* were foreshadowed by Eglantine and Lysiart in Weber's *Euryanthe*.

Because of his political activities and participation in the 1849 uprising in Saxony, Wagner was banished from Germany until 1860. After temporary refuge with his friend Liszt in Weimar, he fled to Switzerland where he wrote his treatises *The Artwork of the Future* (1850) and *Opera and Drama* (1851) which outlined the philosophy and technical methods which were to govern all his subsequent works. He also completed the text for his greatest achievement, *Der Ring des Nibelungen* (The Ring of the Nibelungs), a cycle of four consecutive operas based on the legendary German myths of a primeval power struggle between the Nordic gods led

Richard Wagner (1813–83): caricature entitled 'The Ear of the Universe' published in Paris in 1865

by Wotan and the powers of evil. His aim was to create a complete work of art, a *Gesamtkunstwerk*, in which music, poetry, drama, stage setting, painting, dance and architecture were all to be fused into a single artistic synthesis. Two important influences shaped his creative processes at this time: the philosophy of Schopenhauer and his love for Mathilde Wesendonck, the wife of his friend and patron in Zurich. He broke off his composition of the *Ring* cycle to celebrate their love, doomed to eventual renunciation, in *Tristan und Isolde* (Munich, 1865) which was based on a Celtic legend.

His years of precarious financial insecurity were suddenly ended by the patronage of 19-year-old King Ludwig II of Bavaria (1845–86) who invited him to settle in Munich where he planned to found a music academy and build a festival theatre for the *Ring* cycle. Ludwig's impassioned championship of Wagner aroused jealousy and intrigue within court circles, eventually forcing the composer to return to Switzerland and settle in Triebschen, near Lucerne. His companion was Cosima von Bülow, Liszt's illegitimate daughter, whom he eventually married; *Der Meistersinger von Nürnberg* (Munich, 1868) was written as a celebration of their love.

Ludwig continued his generous financial support and the first two parts of *The Ring*, *Das Rheingold* and *Die Walküre*, were premièred in Munich in 1869 and 1870. The third and fourth parts, *Siegfried* and *Götterdämmerung* (The Twilight of the Gods), were included in the first performance of the complete cycle at the specially built Festspielhaus (Festival Playhouse) at Bayreuth in 1876. His last opera, *Parsifal*, based on the legend of the search for the Holy Grail, was performed there in 1882.

The Festspielhaus was the realisation after quarter of a century of Wagner's dream to design a temple of the arts where his music dramas could be experienced in an almost religious manner, glorifying the new spirit of German nationalism by extolling the myths of her heroic past. *The Ring* is conceived on a vast scale, utilising a far larger orchestra than normal, being submerged and invisible to the audience. Wagner fully exploited it in the use of leitmotivs, themes associated with different characters, events and emotions which act as unifying forces throughout the four parts of the cycle: the water theme of the Rhinemaidens symbolising natural innocence contrasted with Loge's fire music representing evil; the Wanderer motif of Wotan the father god who strives for power without being able to renounce carnal pleasure; the theme of the ring itself, the highest symbol of power, made from the gold stolen from the Rhinemaidens. All who come in contact with the ring are destroyed by its curse which is only lifted by the final realisation that love can overcome power.

Wagner supervised every detail of his elaborate productions and

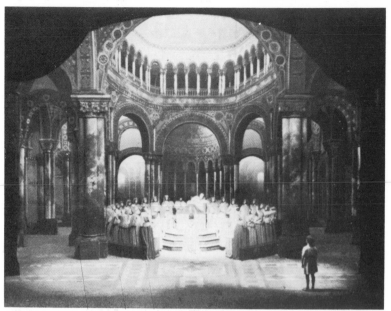

Original 1882 setting of Wagner's Parsifal *at Bayreuth still in use in 1933*

demanded huge voices to ride his torrents of orchestral sound. He used *The Ring* as a vast morality play to preach his theories of good and evil and the final inheritance of the world by a race of Nordic supermen, a belief which subsequently led Hitler and the Third Reich to patronise his works. By a strange irony, the only work by any of his followers to achieve lasting success is *Hänsel und Gretel* (Weimar, 1893), a children's opera by Engelbert Humperdinck (1854–1921).

Nineteenth-century Italian opera

The first half of the nineteenth century saw an enormous growth in the popularity of opera in Italy and also in its commercialisation; the success of a work was no longer determined by the opinion of the aristocrats in the boxes but whether the crowds in the pit and the gallery left a première whistling a new batch of catchy tunes. Gioacchino Rossini (1792–1868) excelled in providing the infectious melodies and sparkling rhythmic vitality that swept an audience off its feet. His first success, *Tancredi* (Venice, 1813), stormed through the Europe of the Napoleonic Wars, making full use of the vogue for rousing military music and gaining Rossini the title 'the Napoleon of music'.

He was engaged as resident composer at the Teatro Argentina in Rome to compose two operas a year and in 1816 *Otello* followed *Il Barbiere di Siviglia* (*The Barber of Seville*, Beaumarchais' story of the events preceding *The Marriage of Figaro*) into production there. The first night of *The Barber of Seville* was a disaster: Count Almaviva broke a guitar string when obliged to tune it for his own serenade, Don Basilio fell through an open trap-door and a cat wandered across the stage. Rossini retired to bed in despair and refused to conduct the second performance when one of the world's supreme comic operas was given a rapturous welcome.

He now started work for the flamboyant impressario Domenico Barbaia (1778–1841), whose mistress, the Spanish soprano Isabella Colbran, he married in 1822. For her he had already written *Elisabetta, Regina d'Inghilterra* (1815) which was loosely based on Sir Walter Scott's novel *Kenilworth* and which set the fashion for English historical operas. He had taken the unprecedented step of writing out all the coloratura decorations in her part; previously singers had improvised their own decorations or made use of those traditionally associated with the role. Rossini also exploited the mezzo coloratura voice for which he wrote leading roles in *La Cenerentola* (Cinderella, 1817), *L'Italiana in Algeri* (The Italian Girl in Algiers, Venice 1813) as well as Rosina in *The Barber of Seville*. As Barbaia was at one time director of the San Carlo in Naples, La Scala in Milan and two opera houses in Vienna, Rossini's successes reached the widest possible audience and ranged from the comedy of *La Gazza Ladra* (The Thieving Magpie, 1817) to serious epics of ancient Egypt and the Old Testament such as *Semiramide* (1823) and *Mosè in Egitto* (Moses in Egypt, 1818).

In 1824 Rossini was appointed director of the Théâtre-Italien in Paris where his four French operas included another scintillating comedy, *Le Comte Ory* (1828), and a grand historical opera appealing to revolutionary fervour, *Guillaume Tell* (William Tell, 1829). Suddenly at the age of 37, after 19 astonishingly fertile years and at the height of his fame, he gave up composing operas, perhaps because of painful gall-stones, perhaps through a reluctance to compete with the rising popularity of Meyerbeer.

He used his influence in Paris to help two of his compatriots gain recognition, Vincenzo Bellini (1801–35), born in Sicily, and

Geraint Evans in Rossini's Barber of Seville, *Covent Garden (1971)*

Gaetano Donizetti (1779–1848), born in Bergamo. Following the success of Victor Hugo's historical dramas, it was no longer obligatory for all operas to have happy endings, and Bellini excelled in writing music for tragic heroines whose sorrows were expressed in melodies of heart-rending beauty; he greatly influenced both Chopin and Liszt. Bellini was fortunate to have as his librettist Felice Romani, who wrote over 90 opera texts and provided him with words ideally suited to the expressiveness of his vocal line; this is displayed in his two best known works, *La Sonnambula* (The Sleepwalker) and *Norma*, both produced in Milan in 1831. When he was invited to compose a work for the Théâtre-Italien, he sought advice from Rossini, and together they revised the finished score of *I Puritani* (The Puritans, Paris 1835). Fortunately he had outstandingly good singers available to do full justice to his *bel canto* style (literally meaning beautiful song) and provide convincingly the larger than life stage portrayals that his tragedies required. Typical of them was the quartet for whom *I Puritani* was written: Grisi, Rubini, Tamburini and the bass Lablache; he was rewriting the role of the heroine Elvira for the soprano Maria Malibran when he suddenly died at the age of 34.

Donizetti was far more prolific and facile in his operatic output, writing more than 70 operas including two enchanting comedies, *L'Elisir d'Amore* (The Elixir of Love, Milan 1832) and *Don*

Pasquale (Paris 1843). His first opera of note was _Anna Bolena_ (Milan 1830), although it was his thirty-fifth composition. His other British inspired operas included _Alfredo il Grande_ (Alfred the Great, Naples 1823), _Emilia di Liverpool_ (Naples 1824) and _Maria Stuarda_ (Naples 1834). Of more lasting fame is _Lucia di Lammermoor_ (Naples 1835), based on Scott's novel _The Bride of Lammermoor_, which Maria Callas revived with outstanding success and which rocketed Joan Sutherland to international stardom. Only a heroine loosing her wits could justify a solo scene of 15 minutes of competitive coloratura with a flute, as in the famous 'mad scene'. To a modern audience _Lucrezia Borgia_ (Milan 1833), based on Hugo's play, seems excessively melodramatic but two of his compositions for Paris, _La Fille du Regiment_ (1840), a comic opera, and _La Favorite_ (1840), a lavish grand opera, make far more interesting revivals.

Verdi

Guiseppe Verdi was born in 1813, the same year as Richard Wagner, and a comparison between these two giant figures of nineteenth-century opera, epitomising the Italian and German traditions, is inevitable. Verdi was a realist whereas Wagner was an idealist. Verdi's themes were the raw stuff of human emotions, the basic passions of love, ambition, jealousy and patriotism; he developed the simplicity of vocal melody to add to recognisable human dilemmas that extra dimension which no straight theatrical performance can equal. Wagner perfected a complex fusion of orchestral sound and sung words to portray the struggle between good and evil in a mythological world. Both fought for their respective country's unification but Verdi remained the champion of the individual whereas Wagner emphasised the progress of national evolution.

Born in poverty in the small village of Le Roncole near Parma, Verdi's first success was _Nabucco_ (Milan 1842) which made him a hero of the Risorgimento, the political movement striving to achieve Italian independence from Austrian rule. His chorus of defeated Israelites expressed the sentiments of a nation united against their oppressors, and also his own despair at the recent tragic deaths of his wife and two young children. His next two operas, _I Lombardi_ (1843) and _Ernani_ (1844), also had revolutionary

Guiseppe Verdi (1813–1901) conducting a performance of Aida

undertones, repeated in *Les Vêpres Siciliennes* (The Sicilian Vespers, Paris 1855) and *Un Ballo in Maschera* (A Masked Ball, Rome 1859) when the patriotic struggle was renewed. *Un Ballo in Maschera* is based on the assassination of King Gustavus III of Sweden, but the censor insisted that Gustavus III be changed to the Earl of Warwick and the opera be set in seventeenth-century Boston. Even in *Rigoletto* (Venice 1851), based on Victor Hugo's play *Le Roi s'amuse*, the names of historical characters, particularly the libertine Francis I of France, had to be changed.

The characterisation, the projection of atmosphere and the removal of the barriers between musical set pieces to provide a continuous musical flow make *Rigoletto* Verdi's first masterpiece. This time he won his battle with the censor over the main character being a deformed hunchback who, at the climax of Piave's excellent libretto, discovers his daughter's dead body in a sack. He was not so fortunate with the adaptation of his next opera *Il Trovatore* (The Troubadour, Rome 1853) in which the melodramatic story of the gypsy insurrectionist who turns out to be the wicked Count's long-lost brother was so drastically compressed that all the linking explanation was left out. Verdi's music sweeps the audience along with its vigorous spontaneity and glorious melody. The dominant figure, the contralto gypsy mother Azucena, follows the example of Meyerbeer's Fidès in *Le Prophète*.

In *La Traviata* (The Woman Who Has Been Led Astray, Venice 1853), Verdi moved away from history and politics to a story of contemporary life based on *La Dame aux Camélias* by Alexander Dumas. The first-night audience balked at the heroine who was both a courtesan and consumptive, particularly when she was played by a large plump prima donna obviously in the rudest of health. With a convincingly slender singer, this delicate drawing room tragedy became one of Verdi's most lasting successes and a vehicle for some of the world's greatest sopranos.

The operas that followed, *Les Vêpres Siciliennes*, *Simon Boccanegra* (Venice 1857), *Un Ballo in Maschera*, *La Forza del Destino* (The Force of Destiny, St Petersburg 1862) and *Don Carlos* (Paris 1867), were like a second apprenticeship in which Verdi refined his musical style, developed orchestral colouring, psychological insight, depth of characterisation and exploited the full potential of melody to intensify the drama of human emotions. *Aida* (Cairo 1871), commissioned by the Khedive of Egypt for the opening of the new

Maria Callas in Verdi's La Traviata *at Covent Garden (1957)*

opera house in Cairo, revealed Verdi at the height of his powers creating the perfect grand opera; spectacular, dramatic, and exotically set in ancient Egypt, the conflict between love and patriotism is brought to its tragic climax without ever sacrificing the humanity of the characters involved.

At the age of 58, Verdi withdrew from the operatic scene to his farm at Saint-Agata and was only persuaded to return after 16 years when, in Arrigo Boito (1842–1918), composer of a highly regarded setting of *Faust* called *Mefistofele* (Milan 1868), he found his ideal librettist. He had already set Shakespeare's *Macbeth* (Florence 1847, revised Paris 1865) and *King Lear* seemed the ideal subject for his old age. This ambition remained unrealised but in its stead Boito provided him with two outstanding libretti which he converted into his final masterpieces, *Otello* (Milan 1887) and *Falstaff* (Milan 1893). The overwhelming tragedy of the jealous Moor was followed by the sparkling comedy of the fat knight at Windsor, his first comic opera since the very beginning of his career. The 80-year-old Verdi brought his great career to a close not with a tragic death scene, but with an irrepressible fugue, 'All the world's a joke!'

Francesco Tamagno as Otello for the first production of Verdi's masterpiece in Milan (1887)

National opera in the nineteenth century

The growth of nationalism in the nineteenth century found vital
expression in music and encouraged the composition of distinctively national operas which combined folk music with familiar
tales of peasant life or well known historical exploits of patriotic
heroes. The most distinctive of these operatic movements to
emerge was that of the Russians.

In the eighteenth century Italian opera made the court of St.
Petersburg indistinguishable from other Western European
capitals; Paisiello, Cimarosa and Salieri were some of the illustri-
ous composers who enjoyed the patronage of Catherine the Great.
At the beginning of the nineteenth century French influence
replaced the Italian when Boïeldieu became conductor of the
Imperial Opera, but as in Weber's Germany, the Romantic
movement stimulated a search for music that would express the
individualistic Russian character rather than blandly conforming
to European fashion.

The first successful attempt to write a truly Russian opera was *A
Life for the Tsar* (originally entitled *Ivan Susanin*) by Mikhail Glinka
(1804–57) which was premièred in St. Petersburg in 1836. Like the
five members of the 'New Russian School' (Balakirev, Cui,
Mussorgsky, Rimsky-Korsakov and Borodin) who came after
him, Glinka was not a professionally trained musician; he was the
son of a land-owning family who started his career in the civil
service and began composing purely as a dilettante to amuse his
lady friends in fashionable drawing rooms. Nicholas I rewarded
Glinka for his patriotic opera, the story of a peasant who sacrificed
his life to save the founder of the Romanov dynasty, with a ring
worth 4,000 roubles and appointed him Master of the Imperial
Chapel. His second opera, *Ruslan and Ludmila* (1842), an exotic
fairy tale poem by Alexander Pushkin (1799–1837), was not so well
received although it formed the basis of a recognisably Russian
style of music and led to his posthumous acclaim both at home and
abroad as the 'Father of Russian Music'.

His style was far removed from the polished niceties of Italian
and French court operas; he was criticised for introducing rough
peasant songs and dances with their strong rhythms, unusual
harmonies and barbaric melodies. His operas also featured superb
choral scenes which made full use of rich Russian basses and he

gave his soloists long lilting melodies with touches of oriental exoticism which recalled the wild tribes of the Caucasus and the Caspian Sea.

Alexander Dargomizhsky (1813–69) concentrated on the dramatic and humorous aspects of Russian folk music in his setting of Pushkin's story *Russalka* (The Water Sprite, 1856). His success in writing dramatic recitative led to the ambitious project of writing an opera in which the music was to follow as closely as possible the inflections of the spoken word – 'melody dictated by meaning'. He chose Pushkin's version of the Don Juan legend, *The Stone Guest* (where would Russian opera be without Pushkin!) and enthralled the 'young lions' gathered round Balakirev. They met regularly at his house to try out episodes of the new opera as soon as they were completed with the composer singing Don Juan, Mussorgsky singing Leporello, Alexandra Purgold singing Laura and Donna Anna, and her sister Nadezdha, the future wife of Rimsky-Korsakov, at the piano. Dargomizhsky died before the work was finished and according to his wishes Cui completed the vocal score and Rimsky-Korsakov orchestrated it for the first performance in 1872. Many of the features which contemporary audiences found unacceptable give a surprisingly modern flavour to this little known work and show its influence on the twentieth-century operas of Prokofiev and Shostakovitch as well as on the greatest of nineteenth century Russian operas, Mussorgsky's *Boris Godunov* (St. Petersburg 1874).

Modest Mussorgsky (1839–81) was a musical amateur, beginning life as a guards officer and then resigning his commission in order to devote himself to composition. In many ways this lack of formal musical training, which Mussorgsky shared with his brothers of the 'Mighty Handful', also known as 'The Five', was an advantage; they were not hampered by traditional German ideas of composition in their struggle to develop a Russian school of opera based on Russian musical and dramatic resources. Mussorgsky was determined in *Boris Godunov* to create an opera which was 'true to life and not melodic in the classical sense'. The work is dominated by the character of the demented Emperor Boris who reigned from 1598 to 1605 and also by the crowd, a group of individuals whom circumstances weld into an overpowering force, the Russian people. The opera is constructed as a series of intense episodes culminating in the death of Boris and the desolation this portends,

Paolo Silveri in a 1948 production of Mussorgsky's Boris Godunov *at Covent Garden*

a very different approach from the gradual unfolding of Wagner's music dramas.

Mussorgsky had great difficulty in getting the work accepted for performance because of its unconventionality, its raw, harsh harmonies, and its expression of popular revolt against despotism, echoing the ideas Tolstoy promulgated after Alexander II freed the serfs. After Mussorgsky's death Rimsky-Korsakov (1844–1908) made *Boris Godunov* more palatable to conventional opera houses by re-orchestrating it and changing the order of the scenes, but since the composer's original score was published in 1928, his own version has been preferred. Rimsky-Korsakov also orchestrated an uncompleted work, *Khovanshchina* (1886), another fiercely national-istic epic describing the conflict between the old feudal regime and new western influences following the accession of Peter the Great.

Rimsky-Korsakov's own operas are in complete contrast to Mussorgsky's tragic and oppressive works. The most successful present a colourful and fantastic land of folk or fairy tale: *The Snow Maiden* (1882), *Sadko* (1898) with its famous 'Hindu Song', and *The Golden Cockerel* (1909). This last, based on Pushkin's satire set in the court of King Dodon, was banned by the censor who thought it a criticism of Nicholas II and the disaster of the Russo–Japanese War. It was eventually performed as a ballet with singers at the side of the stage.

Ballet also played an important part in *Prince Igor* (1890), the opera by which Alexander Borodin (1833–87) is best remembered – the Polovtsian dances from Act II are famous. Borodin was the illegitimate son of a Caucasian prince and made a long study of Central Asiatic themes; he too died leaving his masterpiece to be completed by Rimsky-Korsakov, operatic undertaker to his friends!

In international terms, the most popular and successful Russian composer remains Peter Ilyich Tchaikovsky (1840–93). Although he was on friendly terms with Balakirev's group, he had closer links with the German school led by pianist and composer Anton Rubinstein (1829–94); from 1865 he was professor of harmony at the Moscow Conservatoire headed by Nicholas Rubinstein. His two best operas were based on Pushkin stories, *Eugene Onegin* (Moscow 1879) and *The Queen of Spades* (St. Petersburg 1890). Both feature introspective heroes wracked with tortures of indecision and with whom Tchaikovsky sympathetically identified himself.

Alexander Pushkin

These works are the most successful fusion of Russian musical and literary inspiration with the lyricism of nineteenth-century mainstream opera.

The development of Czechoslovakian music was very similar to that of Russian music. Bedřich Smetana (1824–84) provided the first Czech national opera with *The Bartered Bride* (Prague 1866), a light comic opera exploiting all the richness and colour of Bohemian folk music and peasant life. Of Antonín Dvořák's (1841–1904) ten operas, the only one to approach the popularity of his symphonies outside his native land has been his setting of *Rusalka* (1901).

The founding father of Hungarian opera was Ferenc Erkel (1810–93) whose patriotic works like *Hunyadi László* (1844) and *Bánk Bán* (1861) created a distinctive style. A similar position was held in Poland by Stanislaw Moniuszko (1819–72) after the production of *Halka* in Vilna in 1854.

3

The lighter side – comic opera and operetta

With a tragic story there is no question as to the value of the extra dimension that music can provide, but with a comedy there are more problems. Music may get in the way of words so that verbal jokes fail to come across; attempts to translate comic patter into song may degenerate into meaningless gabble; song is slower than speech, particularly with heavier men's voices, but speed and timing are the essence of verbal wit. One solution is to use spoken dialogue for the jokes and the plot, separating them from the musical numbers which are used in *opera seria* style to illustrate the mood of the characters as the story unfolds. This kind of separation produced French *opéra comique*, English comic opera and German *Singspiel*.

The Italians, particularly the Neapolitans in the eighteenth century, found in *opera buffa* (comic opera) a way of making music an integral part of the comedy. Most of the dialogue was in rapid *recitativo secco* (recitative accompanied only by the harpsichord and perhaps 'cello), but in *La Serva Padrona* (Maid as Mistress) for example, Giovanni Pergolesi (1710–36) uses musical tricks such as sudden off-beat accents, wide leaps and short fussy phrases to characterise grumpy old Uberto, and contrasts them with the charming coquettish melodies, some with a folk song base, for the intriguing young Serpina. These techniques were originally employed for *intermezzi* (interludes) for light relief between the acts of serious operas, but comic operas soon developed into full length works in their own right. A lot of the characters and stock situations were taken from the traditions of *commedia dell'arte* and transferred to the bourgeois world of rich merchants, impudent servants and impoverished young soldiers. Musically, an important development was the grand finale at the end of each act in which all characters joined; this was later adopted by Mozart, Rossini and Verdi.

Niccolò Piccinni (1728–1800) enjoyed great success in Rome with *La Buona Figliuola* (The Good Daughter, 1760), based on Samuel Richardson's novel *Pamela*. The popularity of such light-hearted frolics all over Europe was evidenced by Paisiello's version of *The Barber of Seville*, premièred in St. Petersburg in 1782, and *Il Matrimonio Segreto* (The Secret Marriage) by Domenico Cimarosa (1749–1801) in Vienna in 1792. Among the operas that Joseph Haydn (1732–1809) wrote for his patron Prince Esterhazy were various comedies in the Italian style, including one with a text by Goldoni, *Il Mondo della Luna* (The World on the Moon, 1777).

Although *opera buffa* often parodied the stylised heroics of serious opera, its potential for social and political satire was never developed in the same way as it was by *The Beggar's Opera* in England. The opportunity for criticising one's social superiors by laughing at them in music had to wait until the mid-nineteenth century and the arrival in Paris of Jacques Offenbach (1819–80). Born Jakob Eberst in Cologne, he started his Paris career as a talented 'cellist. He wanted to compose witty musical entertainment and opened his own theatre, 'Les Bouffes-Parisiens', where leaders of Parisian high society could laugh at themselves being lightheartedly caricatured. Indeed the Empress Eugénie referred to the whole brilliant epoch of the Second Empire as 'just one great Offenbach operetta'. Fashionable dances like the gallop and particularly the can-can formed the high spots of the ensembles and sparkling finales of Offenbach's works. Instead of arias and duets to show off great heroic voices as in grand opera, he wrote patter songs to rhyming texts in which it was most important for the audience to understand the words.

His phenomenal output of nearly 100 works for the stage, either full-length operettas or curtain-raisers, included *Orphée aux Enfers* (Orpheus in the Underworld, 1858), a skit on Gluck's *Orfeo ed Euridice*, *La belle Hélène* (1864), *La Vie Parisienne* (1866) and *La Grande Duchesse de Gérolstein* (1867). This last is a marvellous role for a singing actress, originally written for Hortense Schneider who was equally famous for her talents on stage and her love affairs off it. Reputations like hers explain why certain prudish people

Operetta implies spoken dialogue and a sentimental, nostalgic plot.
Opera Buffa - implies resolution, is wittier, & more hardboiled.

Scene from Offenbach's operetta La Belle Hélène *at Sadler's Wells (1963)*

considered operetta to be rather scandalous. The brilliance and vivacity of Offenbach's music is international and timeless and the greatest of his operettas are still as popular today, in modern translations, in London and New York as they were in Paris 100 years ago.

Despite his enormous success, Offenbach hankered for recognition as a composer of grand opera, as did his English counterpart Sir Arthur Sullivan. He did not live to see his aim achieved; *Les Contes d'Hoffmann* (The Tales of Hoffmann), a romantic opera based on the adventures of the German author and composer E. T. A. Hoffmann, was produced a year after his death (1881).

Operetta became so popular that all the great names of French music, including Gounod, Saint-Saëns and Massenet, tried their hand at it for light relief. The two works that have retained their popularity the longest are *La Fille de Madame Angot* (Madame Angot's Daughter, 1872) by Charles Lecocq (1832–1918) and *Véronique* by André Messager (1853–1929).

Offenbach encouraged Johann Strauss (1825–99), the 'waltz king', to translate French operetta using Viennese conventions; the result was *Die Fledermaus* (The Bat, 1874) which has remained an international favourite ever since. The Viennese wanted catchy tunes, frothy stories and plenty of waltzes; theirs was a very different temperament from the Parisians' who delighted in social satire and burlesques of Greek gods and goddesses. Strauss's second most successful operetta was *Der Zigeunerbaron* (The Gypsy Baron, 1885) which has a colourful Hungarian setting; after his death, Adolf Müller concocted a third success, *Wiener Blut* (Viennese Blood, 1899) from some of his best loved music. The 1870s and 1880s were the heyday of Viennese classical operetta. Two composers whom Strauss inspired were Karl Millöcker (1842–99) and Franz von Suppé (1819–95). Favourites by Millöcker are *Der Bettelstudent* (The Beggar Student, 1882) and *Die Dubarry*, while von Suppé's Italian heritage provided the story for his *Boccaccio* (1879). Karl Zeller (1842–98) was another composer whose operetta hits became popular songs in Germany and Austria since his style was much more like folk-song than opera; *Der Vogelhändler* (The Bird Seller, 1891) and *Der Obersteiger* (The Master-miner, 1895) were his greatest successes.

English comic opera

In the ten years following *The Beggar's Opera* 100 ballad operas were produced, all now sunk without trace. Dr. Thomas Arne, of 'Rule Britannia' fame, wrote two charming rustic comedies, *Thomas and Sally* (1760) and *Love in a Village* (1762), with libretti by Isaac Bickerstaffe; Bickerstaffe also wrote for the prolific Charles Dibdin (1745–1814), including *The Padlock* (1768), a Cervantes story featuring a wily black servant named Mungo. Handel was not followed by any English rival to Gluck or Mozart; instead there was an increase in the popularity of charming light works providing entertainment for the pleasure gardens of Vauxhall and Marylebone. Examples of these are Sheridan's *The Duenna* (1775) set to music by his father-in-law Thomas Linley and his son, and *No Song, No Supper* (1790) by Stephen Storace (1763–96), brother of Mozart's first Susanna in *The Marriage of Figaro*.

By far the most lasting and distinctive nineteenth-century English operatic products are the Savoy Operas of Gilbert and

Gilbert and Sullivan's The Gondoliers *at the Savoy Theatre in 1889*

Sullivan, as inimitably English as Offenbach is Parisian or Strauss is Viennese. The stormy partnership between W. S. Gilbert (1836–1911) and Arthur Sullivan (1842–1900), one of Queen Victoria's favourite composers, was like the plot of a comic opera. Their business manager Rupert D'Oyly Carte made a fortune out of their 13 successes produced between 1875 and 1896; he built the Savoy Hotel and Theatre and founded the D'Oyly Carte Opera Company which had sole rights to the performance of the operas until the copyright expired in 1961. Their detractors condemn Gilbert and Sullivan's work as paltry and trivial; their champions know all the words and music by heart and expect them to be performed in exactly the same way as they have been for the past 100 years: Victorian England in aspic.

Gilbert's witty libretti give a unique insight into middle class life and social customs; Sullivan's music is a glorious pastiche of all the popular musical fashions of the day, mixing Verdi, Offenbach and Rossini with his own melodic gifts. Enthusiasts have their favourites from *H.M.S. Pinafore*, *The Pirates of Penzance*, *Patience*, *Iolanthe*, *The Mikado*, *The Yeomen of the Guard* and *The Gondoliers*. They were equally popular in the United States where there were 41 pirated versions of *H.M.S. Pinafore* running within a year of its British première. D'Oyly Carte sent Oscar Wilde to tour the 'Wild

West' mining towns, complete with lily and velvet suit, so that Americans would appreciate the satire of *Patience*.

Gilbert and Sullivan were a hard act to follow but the English taste for light opera was fed by, among others, Sidney Jones (1861–1946), composer of *The Geisha* (1896), Sir Edward German (1862–1936), who wrote *Merrie England* (1902) and Lionel Monckton (1861–1924), best known for *The Quaker Girl*, all providing the necessary pleasing mixture of romantic story and hummable tunes.

4

Opera worldwide

Argentina

A regular opera company was established in Argentina in 1823 and in 1858 the first Teatro Colon, seating 2,500 people, was opened in Buenos Aires. Its greatest season was in 1888 when it starred both Adelina Patti and Francesco Tamagno. An even grander theatre replaced the previous one in 1908 and it has continued to attract the most famous singing stars, conductors and producers of this century. It has always had a close connection with La Scala. During the opening season Chaliapin sang Boito's *Mefistofele*, Toscanini conducted 15 operas in 1912 and Saint-Saëns came to conduct his favourite *Samson et Dalila* in 1916.

From 1925 onwards the theatre has been administered by the municipality and its fortunes have varied according to the political climate. For the fiftieth anniversary of its opening Sir Thomas Beecham conducted the season, including *Otello*, *Carmen*, *Fidelio* and *Die Zauberflöte*, but nothing by an Argentinian composer. Argentinians however have established themselves in the operatic field, starting with Ettore Panizza (1875–1967) with *The Bride of the Sea* (1897) and *Arora* (1908). Arturo Berutti (1862–1938) was the first to write about national subjects in works such as *Los Heroes* (1919); his pupil Felipe Boero was responsible for the first Argentinian opera with a Spanish libretto, *Tucuman*, being performed at the Colon in 1918 and his most successful work, *El Matero* (1929), is based on native folk material. Alberto Ginastera (b. 1916) was commissioned by the Opera Society of Washington, D.C., to write *Bomarzo* (1967) which was subsequently performed by the New York City Center Opera and the English National Opera.

Australia

Australia has been famous for producing fine operatic voices since the days of Dame Nellie Melba. She became very unpopular with her fellow countrymen by advising the great English contralto Clara Butt, about to tour Australia, to 'sing 'em muck!' Perhaps this was a justifiable reflection of the interest which the majority of

Dame Nellie Melba (1861–1931)

Australians had for music in general and opera in particular. The many European refugees who went to Australia just before the Second World War radically changed the situation. National opera companies were founded in Sydney and Melbourne, together with Australian Opera, a touring company founded by the Elizabethan Trust.

After a genesis of nearly 20 years, the Sydney Opera House was opened in 1973; a glorious winged structure designed by the Danish architect Joern Utzon, it is sited on Bennelong Point, a peninsular overshadowed by the Sydney Harbour suspension bridge. Unfortunately the main auditorium, originally designed for opera, was turned into a concert hall and the smaller hall has not the facilities to accommodate a full Wagner orchestra.

The first musical director was the English conductor Edward Downes and the house became a magnet for all the Australian singers who had made their careers in Europe, returning for guest seasons rather than as members of a permanent company. Of leading prominence were Joan Sutherland and her husband Richard Bonynge who is the current musical director. There are also regional companies in Perth, Brisbane, Melbourne and Adelaide, but it is still London to which Australian singers are drawn to make an international career, following in the steps of younger artists like Yvonne Minton and Yvonne Kelly.

Austria

VIENNA STATE OPERA HOUSE
Vienna is perhaps best known for its opera house and its luscious chocolate cake Sacher Torte. Appropriately enough, the Sacher Hotel is built on the site of the old Imperial and Royal Opera House, the Kärntnertor Theatre, which dated from 1763. Here Beethoven conducted the final version of *Fidelio* and the first performance of his Ninth Symphony.

The present system of appointing salaried directors dates only from 1848; before that the Court Opera was leased to administrators who received large subsidies. One of the most colourful lessees was Domenico Barbaia (1778–1841) an ex-waiter and circus proprietor who brought Rossini and his wife, the famous singer Isabella Colbran, from Naples to Vienna and then commissioned Carl Maria von Weber to write *Euryanthe* (1823). In the 1930s he was featured in a comic opera, *Rossini in Neapel* (Rossini arranged by Paumgartner) which even two of the State Opera's most popular male stars, Richard Tauber and Alfred Jerger, failed to make a success.

From 1836 to 1848 the Vienna Opera and La Scala, Milan were under the joint administration of Carlo Balocchino (a maker of pantaloons by profession) and Bartolemo Merelli; they combined the management of opera houses and gambling establishments, a popular nineteenth-century association which today survives only in Monte Carlo. These two Italians brought Donizetti to Vienna as court composer where he composed *Linda di Chamounix* and *Maria di Rohan* followed by the young Verdi who conducted his new opera *Nabucco*. Otto Nicolai (1810–49), engaged as first conductor, failed to have his own opera *The Merry Wives of Windsor* performed, but succeeded in transforming the Court Opera Orchestra into the Vienna Philharmonic (1842).

The new Imperial Opera House, opened in 1869, was conceived as one of the crowning glories of the Ringstrasse, which replaced the old city gates and fortifications and was built as a monument to Emperor Franz Josef's power and magnificence. The two architects who won the competition to design the house did not live to see it completed. Malicious criticism drove Eduard Van der Nüll to suicide, and his friend and colleague August von Siccardsburg died a broken man a few months after him. Their creation proved to be a superb success with almost perfect acoustics, and for the next 40 years reflected the opulent heyday of the Austro-Hungarian Empire.

Johann Herbeck (1831–77) was the first star conductor to become director of the Vienna Opera. During the first Viennese performance of *Die Meistersinger* feeling between the pro- and anti-Wagner factions rose so high that the Hans Sachs, Johann N. Beck, lost his voice with fright and Herbeck had to sing as well as conduct! Vienna's conversion to Wagner was completed by Franz Jauner who engaged Hans Richter to conduct and brought Wagner himself to supervise productions of *Tannhäuser* and *Lohengrin*. Jauner produced *Die Walküre* with Wagner's favourite Brünnhilde, Amelie Materna, a statuesque soprano from Styria, and real horses ridden by Polish horsemen dressed as the Valkyries' doubles. Wilhelm Jahn, director from 1881 to 1897, successfully held the position longer than anyone else. Concentrating on the

Vienna Imperial Opera House in the 1880s

Gustav Mahler (1860–1911)

French and Italian repertoire, he premièred Massenet's *Werther* in 1892 and introduced the *verismo* operas of Mascagni and Leoncavallo. His leading romantic singers were Marie Renard and Ernest van Dyk, part of an ensemble of world class artists who were under sole contract to his opera house.

He was followed by Gustav Mahler (1860–1911), who during his ten years of turbulent reign revolutionised the repertoire according to the concept of 'total theatre' inspired by the Swiss stage designer Adolphe Appia. With the painter Alfred Roller in charge of lighting and set design he devised new productions of all the great German operas, taking most of the piano rehearsals as well as producing and conducting. He insisted on musical accuracy and precision and assembled a team of fanatically dedicated singers led by Selma Kurz, Anna Mildenburg, Erik Schmedes, Richard Mayr and the giant heroic tenor Leo Slezak from Brno who outsang all rivals for 33 years.

Felix von Weingartner (1863–1942) was hailed as the champion of the anti-Mahler clique when the daemonic composer/conductor finally departed for the New York Metropolitan opera, wearied by intrigue and criticisms of over-spending. In 1910 the première of *Der Schneeman* (The Snowman), written by 11-year-old Erich Wolfgang Korngold (1897–1957), was given; his early recognition was due to his father being one of Vienna's most powerful music critics.

Hans Gregor was the first opera director of the modern 'manager' type (1911–18). He introduced to Vienna three of the most popular stage idols it has ever known. Maria Jeritza from Brno in Czechoslovakia had great beauty, a radiant voice and a hypnotic stage personality. Puccini's favourite Tosca, she was the first to sing 'Vissi d'arte, vissi d'amore' (Love and music I lived for) lying flat in supplication on the floor. Her popular partner in Vienna was the English-born tenor Alfred Piccaver, who had a voice of satin heightened by a nasal brilliance. The rival leading lady was Lotte Lehmann who excelled in the warmer roles of loving help-mate in contrast to the *femme fatale*. She also became a great favourite at the Metropolitan opera and ended her long life as a distinguished teacher in Santa Barbara, California.

The reign of the Austro-Hungarian Empire's double-headed imperial eagle ended on 10 November 1918 and the first triumph for the Vienna State Opera was the world première of Richard

Covent Garden production of Richard Strauss's Die Frau ohne Schatten *(1967)*

Strauss's opera *Die Frau ohne Schatten* (The Woman without a Shadow) with Jeritza, Lehmann and Mayr leading the cast. Two months later Strauss was appointed joint director with Franz Schalk. Far less demanding than Mahler, Strauss was subjected to similar intrigue, to criticism of his pleasure-giving approach to music and for including too many of his own operas in the programme; he resigned in 1924, leaving Schalk as sole director from 1924 to 1929. Some of the singers Strauss fostered included Elisabeth Schumann, Rosette Anday, Jan Kiepura and Richard Tauber. Strauss supported the appointment of Clemens Krauss (1929–34) who proved to be the Opera's most dynamic director since Mahler. He also gathered a group of singers and an outstanding producer, Lother Wallerstein, dedicated to him and his ideals. Until 1938 the Vienna State Opera was able to engage artists forced to leave Germany by its racial laws, and in 1936 Bruno Walter was appointed artistic director.

The State Opera House was one of the final casualties of the Second World War; the stage, auditorium and rehearsal rooms were completely burnt out. Until the theatre was rebuilt and reopened in November 1955, externally a replica of its former grandeur and internally benefitting from all the most modern developments in technical equipment, the Vienna State Opera found a temporary home in the Theater an der Wien and the Volksoper. The roster of singers who consolidated the international fame of the Vienna State Opera included Elisabeth Schwarzkopf, Irmgard Seefried, Lisa della Casa, Sena Jurinac, Hans Hotter, Paul Schöffler and Anton Dermota, conducted by Joseph Krips, Carl Böhm and Herbert von Karajan.

From 1956 to 1964 when Karajan was artistic manager, the Vienna State Opera enjoyed a new 'golden age'. He introduced a policy of international super-productions sung by jet-age stars, the highest paid singers in the world, jointly available to Vienna and La Scala, Milan. The supreme autocrat, he was a meticulous producer as well as an electrifying conductor. His personal charisma has been challenged only by Leonard Bernstein who became Vienna's new idol in 1966.

In 1982 another American, Lorin Maazel, took up the post of chief conductor, overseeing a repertoire of approximately 50 standard works and a ten-month season.

THEATER AN DER WIEN

Built by Emanuel Schikaneder (Mozart's librettist for *The Magic Flute*), the Theater an der Wien opened in 1801 and gave the première of *Fidelio* in 1805. Later in the nineteenth century it became the home of Viennese operetta; 13 of Johann Strauss's works had their first performance there, as did Lehar's *The Merry Widow* and *The Count of Luxembourg*. Since its reopening in 1962 it has been used for operas during the Vienna Festival and otherwise for musicals and operetta.

VOLKSOPER

Built in 1898 to be a people's opera house commemorating the fiftieth anniversary of Franz Joseph's reign, the Volksoper launched the careers of many singers who later progressed to the State Opera House. From 1955 its policy was to revive Viennese operetta and recreate the American musical in German, but it is now Vienna's second opera house for standard repertoire.

REDOUTENSAAL

Originally part of the ceremonial state apartments in the Imperial Hofburg (Royal Court), the Redoutensaal was taken over by the Vienna State Opera in 1921 and is a delightful setting for Mozart and Rossini operas.

SALZBURG

The first Salzburg Festival took place in 1920 and included Max Reinhardt's production of Hugo von Hofmannsthal's *Jederman* (Everyman) in the Cathedral Square and this has remained an annual, central feature. The tradition of Mozart concerts and operas was established by Bernhard Paumgartner who was a guiding force of the festival for over 40 years. In 1926 open air opera performances were started in the Felsenreitschule (Summer Riding School) and the high artistic standards of the festival were set by Richard Strauss, Franz Schalk and Alfred Roller. In the 1930s leading conductors included Bruno Walter, Toscannini, Furtwängler and Knappertsbusch with Herbert Graf as producer. Since the Second World War the most brilliant festival director has been Karajan.

Graz, Austria's second largest city, and Linz, on the Danube, have the most important provincial opera houses in Austria, providing a springboard for young artists.

Eastern Europe

Czechoslovakia continues the flourishing operatic tradition consolidated by Smetana and Dvořák whose works remain the most popular in the repertoire, not only in Prague but in the seven or eight regional companies including Ostrava, Plzeň, Olomouc and Brno. Brno became the home town of Leoš Janáček (1854–1928) whose international reputation has continued to increase since his death. His musical style is closely linked to the Czech language but his operas have been successfully translated into English and German. His best known works include *Jenůfa* (1904), *Kátya Kabanová* (1921), *The Cunning Little Vixen* (1924) and *From the House of the Dead* (1930) based on Dostoyevsky's novel.

Operatic life in Hungary, Poland, Rumania and Yugoslavia also flourishes with state run repertory companies performing a limited repertoire but including some Italian and German classical operas in the original language. Very few contemporary works by Eastern Bloc composers, apart from the East Germans, are heard in the West. One exception is the Polish composer Krzystof Penderecki whose opera *The Devils of Loudon* was performed by the English National Opera in 1973. No Hungarian composer has approached the importance of Béla Bartók (1881–1945) whose only opera is the disturbingly effective Freudian one act work *Duke Bluebeard's Castle* (Budapest 1918). Bulgaria has produced two of the finest post war basses in Boris Christoff and Nicholai Ghuiarov.

Because of currency problems the exchange of singers between countries in Eastern and Western Europe is limited; unless they can be paid in foreign currency, English singers invited to Czechoslovakia, for example, find that they cannot exchange their fees except for cut glass and teddy bears! The currency earnings of Eastern European singers in the West are very welcome to their governments but their artistic freedom and choice of engagements tend to be limited by political considerations.

France

PARIS OPÉRA

The Théâtre de l'Opéra was opened in 1875 and remains one of the major sights of Paris, being the most lavish and ornate opera house in the world. The major triumphs of the Paris Opéra in the nineteenth century, the spectacular successes of Meyerbeer, Halévy and Verdi's *Don Carlos*, took place at the Rue le Peletier in the twelfth opera house to be built there since the Académie Royale de Musique was opened in 1669. On their way to a gala night there in January 1858, a bomb destroyed the carriage of Napoleon III and Empress Eugénie, who miraculously remained unhurt although their coachman was killed and over 150 people badly injured. The Emperor decreed that a new opera house should be built north of the Place de la Concorde in isolated magnificence to avoid another assassination attempt. The winner of the competition for its design was Charles Garnier who described his building's grandiose style as 'Second Empire', but by the time it was opened Napoleon III had died in exile and France was a republic again. The distinguished inaugural gathering included the Lord Mayor of London with his gilt coach, trumpeters and Master of the Poultry!

Known as the Palais Garnier, Debussy rudely commented that the vast edifice 'looks like a railway station; inside one might be forgiven for thinking it was the central lounge of a turkish bath.' The grand staircase and foyers are extremely flamboyant, every surface being covered with intricate decoration and now surmounted by Chagall's painted ceiling 'Bouquet de Rêves'. There are

Paris Opéra in 1875

1,606 doors, 6,319 steps and 334 dressing rooms; before lifts were installed it used to take singers and orchestral players up to an hour to get to their rehearsal rooms.

From 1884 to 1908 Pedro Gailhard was director of the Opéra with a conventional repertoire of box-office favourites led by Gounod's *Faust* and *Roméo et Juliette*. By the end of 1970 *Faust* had been given 2,383 times at the Opéra. When he staged Wagner's *Lohengrin* in 1891 anti-German feeling ran so high that stink bombs were thrown. The only world premières of note during this period were Massenet's *Le Cid* (1885) and *Thaïs* (1894). It was only in 1905 that the name of the conductor started to appear on the programmes; until then he had sat beside the prompter's box with his back to the musicians.

In 1908 the composer and conductor André Messager (1853–1929) was appointed to the Opéra; best known for his operetta *Véronique*, he had previously managed Covent Garden. Ironically his production of *Parsifal* was a great success in the year that Germany again declared war on France. By this time the claque had at last officially disappeared from the Opéra – unofficially it survived until 1939. This age old institution was a specially recruited group who could ensure the success or ruin of any performance by being paid to applaud or deride it. The *Chef de*

Claque started up vociferous approval for any singer prepared to pay 150 francs a time.

From 1914 to the Second World War the Opéra was fortunate enough to have a director who was also a very wealthy business man, Jacques Rouché, head of Parfumerie Pinat, who paid the annual deficit out of his own pocket. In 25 years he presented 71 operas and 73 ballets including the premières of two works by Darius Milhaud (1892–1975): *Maximilien* (1932) and *Medée* (1940). His better known works were premièred elsewhere including *L'enlèvement d'Europe* (The Rape of Europa, Baden-Baden 1927), *Christophe Colombe* (Berlin 1930) and *David* (Milan 1955). He was one of *Les Six*, the leading group of French avant-garde composers formed in the 1920s which included Arthur Honegger (1892–1955) who was of Swiss parentage. Honegger's first successes were *Le Roi David*, performed as an opera at Mézières in 1921 and subsequently given as an oratorio all over the world, and *Judith* staged at Monte Carlo in 1926. His best known dramatic oratorio *Jeanne d'Arc au Bûcher* (Joan of Arc at the Stake) was first given in Zurich in 1942.

During the German occupation of Paris, Hitler took over the Opéra, and *Die Fledermaus* was staged for his troops. When it was reopened after the war it was as a state institution. Its first memorable triumph was a spectacular baroque production of *Les Indes Galantes* by Rameau in 1952, followed by Birgit Nilsson as Turandot in a production by Margherita Wallmann, the outstanding woman producer of her generation. One of the high points during the administration of Georges Auric, a surviving member of *Les Six*, was Berg's *Wozzeck* conducted by Pierre Boulez who was equally famous as conductor and avant-garde composer during the post-war period.

In 1973 a new era began at the Paris Opéra under the Swiss composer Rolf Liebermann, who came from Hamburg, as administrator and Georg Solti as artistic advisor. It was ushered in with an impressive production of Schoenberg's *Moses and Aaron* in 1974 and the commissioning of an opera from France's most highly acclaimed modern composer, Olivier Messiaen (b. 1908). In 1980 Bernard Lefort and Silvio Varvisi were appointed as administrator and artistic advisor.

OPÉRA-COMIQUE

Because of the French distinction between *opéra comique* works with spoken dialogue and grand opera in which everything is sung, many of the best known French operas were never performed at the Théâtre de l'Opéra but always at the Opéra-Comique. The actual theatre in the Rue Favart where *Carmen* was premièred was burnt down in 1887 and reopened in 1898. It was here that Claude Debussy (1862–1918) launched his great impressionistic opera, *Pélleas et Mélisande*, to Maurice Maeterlinck's libretto in 1902. The Opéra-Comique's second internationally successful work was in a completely different vein; a one-act comedy, *L'Heure Espagnole* (The Spanish Hour), by Maurice Ravel (1875–1937) was premièred in 1911.

Ravel's second success, *L'Enfant et les Sortilèges* (The Child and the Enchantments), is a charming setting of Colette's story about a naughty child who is terrorised by the nursery toys he has ill-treated and was first performed at the Monte Carlo Opera House in 1925.

In 1939 the Opéra-Comique was joined with the Opéra under state supervision, pooling their orchestras and repertoire. *Carmen* remained the prerogative of the Opéra-Comique but a sparkling 1959 production starring Jane Rhodes and Albert Lance and

Sadler's Wells production of Maurice Ravel's L'Heure Espagnole *(1966)*

conducted by the young Roberto Benzi was transferred to the Opéra for a state visit by General de Gaulle. After the disturbances of 1968/9 in Paris, the Opéra-Comique was closed, and in 1971 was reorganised as the Opéra-Studio to train singers, conductors and producers and give small-scale performances.

MONTE CARLO

The Monte Carlo Opera House opened four years after the Paris Opéra and was designed by Charles Garnier who had been commissioned to build a similarly ornate theatre to display the opulence of the Principality of Monaco. For more than 50 years it flourished under the directorship of Raoul Gunsbourg (1859–1955), a Rumanian who produced the first stage performance of Berlioz's *Le Damnation de Faust* in 1893, a number of Massenet premières and Puccini's least successful work, *Le Rondine* (The Swallow), in 1917.

THE PROVINCES

Opera has enjoyed a long and well-established tradition in the French provinces. There are now 14 opera houses grouped together within the Réunion des Théâtres Lyriques Municipaux de France and catering, despite financial stringencies, for a growing opera public. The cities of Colmar, Mulhouse and Strasbourg are grouped together as the Opéra du Rhin; other main centres include Bordeaux, Lyon, Marseille, Nice, and Toulouse.

Because of the very specialised characteristics of the French language, particularly its precise vowels, forward placing and nasal quality, French singing differs greatly from Italian, German, Russian or English singing. This makes it difficult for foreigners to give completely authentic sounding performances in French opera, although Debussy chose the Scots-born Mary Garden to be his first Mélisande because of the attractiveness of her slight accent, a trait shared with his second choice, English-born Maggie Teyte. Conversely French singers in general do not excel in the music of other languages; notable exceptions have included Régine Crespin.

Germany

The state of opera in West Germany is totally different from that in any other country, both in volume and quality of production and performance. There are as many as 54 theatres giving a regular season of opera and operetta, quite apart from summer seasons and open air performances. This musical superabundance dates from the political fragmentation of Germany before 1871, when every princedom, dukedom, archbishopric and city state had its own theatre as a status symbol, and each vied with its neighbour in the splendour of its operatic productions. Today's theatres vary in size from those of world rank such as Hamburg, Berlin, Cologne, Frankfurt, Stuttgart and Munich, to small provincial houses such as Flensburg, Detmold or Trier. Whether their budgets range from 6 million to 50 million Deutschmarks a year, they are all financed from public funds and provide ten-month seasons amounting to more than 200 performances each a year.

Most of the theatre companies are three-part, providing drama and ballet as well as opera, operetta and musicals, and they usually have a smaller theatre for drama and a studio for experimental theatre, leaving the large house free for music. Most theatres also provide touring performances for the surrounding areas; Flensburg for example, Germany's northern-most opera house, provides productions for the German speaking minority of Nord Schleswig in Denmark.

Apart from the houses of international repute, the repertoire is all sung in German, but many of the singers are not German. As many as 40 per cent of theatre employees, particularly singers, conductors and instrumentalists, are foreigners; the highest proportion of soloists and conductors come from America, chorus singers from Eastern Bloc countries and orchestral players from Japan. Over the years complaints from German artists and theatre unions have increased, but attempts to limit the proportion of foreigners in an ensemble have foundered on the problem of supply and demand. There are just not enough German artists of a high enough standard to fill all the vacancies. America, with its plethora of music faculties and university opera workshops, produces excellent and experienced young opera singers with no possibility of regular professional employment at home. They crowd the German agents' offices and are snapped up by small opera houses as beginners on minimal salaries.

With excellent productions of opera and operetta on television, local audiences expect a high standard of performance from their own theatre, however small. A German beginner going to his first engagement straight from music college is not going to have the experience or stamina for three performances of Radames and two of Manrico in a week if both *Aida* and *Il Trovatore* are in repertoire; however, an American or British tenor, already with substantial experience at home, will be willing to take on this 'make or break' feat in order to get his foot on the German operatic ladder. Artists are usually contracted for one or two years for the season starting each August. German audiences have become used to their language being abused on stage by foreign singers; after all, the music is more important than the words. Problems arise, however, in operetta and works like *Zar und Zimmermann* (by Albert Lortzing) which have spoken dialogue. The shortage of German singers is due to a lack of sufficiently good training and prejudice against music as a profession. Very few singers can hope to attain the glamorous heights of being a star; on the lower slopes, the physical and emotional demands are just as punishing, but the social status is lacking and the annual salary is about 35 per cent lower than that of other professions which demand an equally long and intensive training.

Only 15 per cent of the annual theatre budget comes from box office sales; the majority of tickets are sold on the *Abonnement* system in which season tickets cover a number of different productions throughout the year, often being sold to factories, churches or community associations. German provincial theatres provide a social and cultural centre for the whole area, and because it is not seen as an upper-class or elitist entertainment there is no stigma against opera. The same broad section of the community enjoys *Carmen* and *The Magic Flute* as *Kiss me Kate* or *Blume von Hawaii* (Abraham). Because the theatre relies on public subsidy for most of its revenue and is subject to a certain amount of local political pressure, the repertoire tends to be safe rather than adventurous. With few exceptions one will find the same acceptable diet of Mozart, Verdi, Puccini and Richard Strauss all over Germany without many excursions into contemporary opera. One of the most adventurous German works of the last 20 years, *Die Soldaten* by Bernd Alois Zimmermann (1918–70), has only been performed in six large houses since its 1965 première in Cologne. West Germany's two most successful opera composers of the postwar generation, Giselher Klebe and Hans Werner Henze, rarely have their works performed in German provincial opera houses.

Richard Strauss (1864–1949) c. *1890*

HAMBURG

By the 1870s, the Hamburg Town Theatre had fallen on hard days; it was bought up by a share company for one million Reichsmarks and leased out to Bernhard Pohl, an experienced impresario known professionally as Pollini. Having remodelled and modernised the theatre, he raised the ticket prices and established a company of gifted young singers, nurturing their careers so that Hamburg became the departure point for Vienna for great Wagnerian singers like contralto Ernestine Schumann-Heink, baritone Eugen Gura and soprano Rosa Sucher. The climax of his long directorship came during the six years (1891–98) when Gustav Mahler was musical director and Alfred Roller was designer and producer. Apart from engaging Mahler's protégé, the young Otto Klemperer, musical standards fell after Pollini's death, but the cult of the singer continued and the house's rising stars included Lotte Lehmann and Elisabeth Schumann.

The rise of the Nazi régime had the same effect in Hamburg as throughout German cultural life: works by Jewish composers disappeared from the repertoire and Jewish artists were dismissed to be replaced by acceptable establishment figures of mediocre talent. Notable exceptions were chief conductor Eugen Jochum and chief producer Oscar Fritz Schuh whose merits found further recognition in the post-war era.

Until the theatre on the Dammtorstrasse was rebuilt and reopened in 1955, the company, under the directorship of Günther Rennert, had to make do with temporary premises and minimum facilities. These produced a new operatic style, stripping away the externals of lavish costumes and sets and concentrating instead on the original intentions of the composer as interpreted by the individual producer. Rennert had a very distinctive personal style, particularly with Mozart operas. Carl Ebert developed a similar new style in Berlin at the Deutsche Oper's temporary home, the Theater des Westens, from 1954 to 1961.

Rennert also brought into the Hamburg repertoire the kind of modern works which had been banned during the Third Reich, including Stravinsky, Hindemith, Berg and Schoenberg. From 1959 to 1973 Rolf Liebermann (b. 1910), himself a distinguished opera composer, was director. He consolidated Hamburg's position as a leading international opera house by importing top international stars as guests, some contracted for a certain number of performances during the year, to work with the permanent company which had a few celebrity singers under regular contract and rising young performers available for smaller roles and repertory productions. Today this is the general international pattern which tends to lead to first and second league performances, top prices being charged for the visiting attractions and lower prices for the home company's appearances.

Liebermann took the Hamburg company on prestige visits to Edinburgh, Paris, Montreal and New York. More importantly for the development of contemporary music theatre, he produced the première of a commissioned work every year; these included Gunther Schuller's *The Visitation*, Krzystof Penderecki's *The Devils of Loudon* and Alexander Goehr's *Arden Must Die*. His successor, August Everding, opened a small experimental theatre so that newly commissioned works now reach a smaller audience.

The present general administrator is the conductor Christoph von Dohnanyi who had previously built up the Frankfurt company, following the reputation it had established under Georg Solti in the 1950s. The Frankfurt board of directors is now led by Christoph Bitter and Michael Gielen, the latter being one of the leading conductors of contemporary music. Unlike Cologne and Düsseldorf where most artists appear as guests, Nuremberg has a company composed of soloists who are all under regular contract to the house. It was the first theatre to introduce American musicals such as *West Side Story*, *My Fair Lady* and *Fiddler on the Roof* which are now established repertoire favourites throughout Germany.

STUTTGART

The Württemberg State Theatre, which reopened in 1949, has 200 years of operatic tradition behind it. Under the directorship of Walter Erich Schäfer until 1971, a very strong company was developed, with Ferdinand Leitner as musical director and many productions by Günther Rennert and Wieland Wagner. These included so many Wagner works that it became known as the 'Winter Bayreuth'. The company included the two great tenors Wolfgang Windgassen and Fritz Wunderlich. Under the inspiration of the Australian choreographer John Cranko, an outstanding ballet company was established; previously ballet had been a sadly neglected field in Germany.

Munich's Nationaltheater as it was before the Second World War

MUNICH

The most beautiful theatre in Munich is unquestionably the Cuvillés, built in 1775 within the royal palace of the Wittelbachs. During the Second World War the elaborate rococo decoration of the interior was removed for safe keeping so that when it was rebuilt in 1958 on a different site, it reopened looking very much as it had done for the première of Mozart's *Idomeneo* in 1781.

The Nationaltheater, first built in 1811, has an impressive classical facade modelled on the Paris Odeon and is the work of Karl von Fischer whose wife was an opera singer. It was here that the first performances of four Wagner operas took place, beginning with *Tristan und Isolde* in 1865 conducted by Franz Lachner. Lachner was followed by musicians of the eminence of Hans von Bülow, Hermann Levi, Felix Mottl and Richard Strauss; after the First World War their place was taken by Bruno Walter, Hans Knappertsbusch and Clemens Krauss, who provided the libretto for Strauss's opera *Capriccio* which was premièred in Munich in 1942. A previous Strauss première had been *Friedenstag* (The Day of Peace) in 1938. Hans Pfitzner provided (1869–1949) another important Munich première with *Palestrina* in 1917.

The Prinzregententheater opened in 1901 and, modelled on the Bayreuth Festspielhaus, was intended only for a Wagner festival to be held in August and September. It was the eventual realisation of

Mad King Ludwig II's desire for a festival theatre for Wagner's operas, but was not the grandiose project he had dreamed of above the River Isar.

After the damage to the Nationaltheater in the Second World War, the Prinzregententheater became the main Munich opera house under the direction of Rudolph Hartmann. Despite its restricted space, a high standard of performance was developed under conductors like Georg Solti, Herbert von Karajan, Rudolph Kempe and Ferenc Fricsay. The reconstructed Nationaltheater was opened in 1963, the biggest opera house in West Germany with over 2,000 seats. Wolfgang Sawallisch succeeded Joseph Keilberth as musical director and for nine years Günther Rennert was director, followed by August Everding; top administrative positions in German opera houses are rather like musical chairs! For singers, there is a well marked ladder to climb from the small provincial house, through the middle range like Brunswick, Bremen and Mannheim to the eight or ten top ranking houses. But there is of course no guarantee that the talented young beginner in Trier will ever get to the Bavarian State Opera in Munich.

At the end of the season, the Munich Opera Festival, not to be confused with the beer celebrations of the Oktoberfest, presents the world's most famous singers in a guest company which includes German singers like Dietrich Fischer-Dieskau, Hermann Prey, Theo Adam, Helga Doenesch and Brigitte Fassbaender. Like the uniformity of international hotels found in the world's main cities, it is only the language of the audience and the decoration of the auditorium which distinguishes Munich from Milan or New York when Montserrat Caballé and Placido Domingo are singing *La Traviata* or Birgit Nilsson and Jon Vickers are in *Tristan and Isolde*.

Munich's second opera company has its home in the State Theatre on the Gärtnerplatz; specialising in operetta and musicals in a similar way to the Vienna Volksoper, it now also includes standard works from the opera repertoire in German.

Two of West Germany's most successful opera composers of the older generation are South Germans and started their careers in Munich. Werner Egk's best known operas include *Die Zaubergeige* (The Magic Violin, Frankfurt 1935), *Der Revisor* (The Government Inspector, Schwetzingen Festival 1957) and *Die Verlobung in San Domingo* (The Betrothal in San Domingo) written for the reopening of the Nationaltheater in 1963. Carl Orff's most popular work is a scenic cantata, *Carmina Burana* (Frankfurt 1937), and his most theatrically successful is the fairy tale opera *Die Kluge* (The Clever Woman, Frankfurt 1943). He has also applied his highly individual style to settings of Greek tragedies such as *Antigonae* (Salzburg 1949).

BERLIN

Opera in Berlin is obviously complicated by the division of the city into East and West. The State Opera House was originally the Court Opera built in the famous Unter den Linden in 1742 for Frederick the Great of Prussia; it was here that German Romantic opera was founded with the première of Weber's *Der Freischütz* in 1821. Early in the twentieth century its chief conductors were Weingartner, Muck and Strauss, followed by Kleiber, who in 1929 conducted the première of *Wozzeck*, Alban Berg's (1885–1935) masterpiece, and in 1930 premièred *Christophe Colomb* by Darius Milhaud (1892–1974). The young Herbert von Karajan first made his mark in the house which from 1927 to 1945 had Heinz Tietjen as administrator, producer and conductor.

The Berlin State Opera attained such symbolic significance during the Nazi era that when it was bombed in 1941 it was rebuilt, at the command of the supreme chief of Prussian theatres, Field Marshal Goering, in even greater splendour for a sumptuous production of *Die Meistersinger* conducted by Wilhelm Furtwängler; it was destroyed again in 1945. When the company returned to a rebuilt theatre ten years later it was situated in East Berlin. The repertoire has remained conventional and the performances are sound and competent if somewhat unexciting. There is a strong obligation to foster contemporary works, the most successful of which have been those of Paul Dessau (1894–1979), including *The Trial of Lucullus* (1951), to a libretto by Berthold Brecht, *Puntila* and *Lanzelot*.

By far the most exciting productions in Berlin, both East and West, are to be found at the Komische Oper founded in 1947 by Walter Felsenstein. Felsenstein was incredibly painstaking and would work with his company of singer/actors for up to two years on a production before he was satisfied that the result fulfilled the dramatic truth of the work and was ready for the public. His most famous productions ranged from Monteverdi's *Il Ritorno d'Ulisse in*

Otto Klemperer (1885–1973)

Patria and Mozart's *Die Zauberflöte* to Bizet's *Carmen*, Janáček's *The Cunning Little Vixen* and Britten's *A Midsummer Night's Dream*. His theories are now being disseminated throughout the world's opera houses by two of his most brilliantly gifted protégés, Götz Friedrich and Joachim Herz.

The Komische Oper has been compared with the most stimulating operatic experiment in Berlin between the two world wars, at the Kroll Theatre under Otto Klemperer. Started in 1927 as a criticism of standard repertory productions, the idea was to provide an opera house for members of the Free People's Theatre (*Freie Volksbühne*), a working class movement, and also to interest the kind of intellectuals who condemned opera as conventional and uninteresting. Klemperer insisted on a professor of art, Ewald Dülberg, as his stage director and an art historian/musicologist, Dr Hans Cujel, as his literary adviser (*dramaturg*) and producer. Schoenberg's brother-in-law, Alexander von Zemlinsky (also a composer), and Fritz Zweig were the conductors for a young and dedicated company of singers without any stars. Following *Fidelio*, a fairly traditional repertoire was developed but it was presented in a new and challenging way by theatre producers like Gustav Gründgens, modern painters of the stature of László Moholy-

Nagy and Giorgio de Chirico, and stage designers like Theo Otto and Caspar Neher. A whole new style of dramatic interpretation and stage movement was evolved for the singers as well.

Artistically the Kroll was a magnificent success and quite rehabilitated opera in the eyes of the intellectual bourgeoisie; the working classes of the Free People's Theatre found it somewhat over their heads. The changing political situation, however, spelt its downfall; the Kroll was accused of 'cultural Bolshevism' and closed down in 1931.

Meanwhile a more conventional type of opera was being performed by the Deutsches Opernhaus with Bruno Walter conducting and Carl Ebert producing an ensemble that included Maria Ivogün, Lotte Lehmann and Sigrid Onegin. When the theatre was reopened as the German Opera of West Berlin in 1961, Gustav Sellner continued Carl Ebert's concentration on Mozart and Verdi operas but he also brought in works by Berg, Hindemith, Orff and Schoenberg and premières of Egk, Henze, Boris Blacher and Luigi Dallopiccola. Despite the prestige of Lorin Maazel, musical director until 1971, and Siegfried Palm, director since 1976, it has proved very difficult for the German Opera in West Berlin to develop a distinctive house personality and style.

EAST GERMANY

Apart from Berlin, the two main opera centres of East Germany are Dresden and Leipzig. The citizens of Dresden have long been renowned for their love of opera, even before Carl Maria von Weber took charge of the German Musical Department of the Royal Saxon Theatre in 1817. A new opera house designed by Gottfried Semper was opened in time for the première of Wagner's *Rienzi* (1842), and following its success Wagner was appointed musical director, himself conducting the first performances of *The Flying Dutchman* (1843) and *Tannhäuser* (1845). The third personality in Dresden's operatic life was Ernst von Shuch who took over Semper's rebuilt theatre which was opened in 1878. He began the twentieth century with the first of a series of brilliant Richard Strauss premières: *Feuersnot* (1901), *Salome* (1905), *Elektra* (1909), and *Der Rosenkavalier* (1911). The Strauss tradition was continued by Fritz Busch, with premières of *Intermezzo* (1924) and *Die Ägyptische Helena* (1928). He built up an ensemble of young singers including Elisabeth Rethberg, Erna Berger and Paul Schöffler, and expanded the repertoire of contemporary works by staging premières of *Cardillac* (1926) by Paul Hindemith (1895–1963), *Doktor Faust* (1925) by Ferruccio Busoni (1866–1924) and *Der Protagonist* (1926) by Busoni's pupil Kurt Weill (1900–50). The National Socialists forced Busch out of office so that the première of Strauss' *Arabella* (1933) was conducted by Clemens Krauss and those of *Die Schweigsame Frau* (1935) and *Daphne* (1938) were conducted by Karl Böhm.

In 1945, like so many of Germany's opera houses, the theatre was destroyed; since the war, one theatre has been shared between opera and drama. Conductors have included Joseph Keilberth, Lovro von Matačić and Kurt Sanderling, with Dresden-born Peter Schreier and Theo Adam leading the ensemble of singers. In 1975 Herbert Blomstedt was appointed chief conductor of the State Opera and the 400-year-old Dresden Orchestra, which remains 'the miraculous harp' eulogised by Wagner.

Leipzig has not had to wait as long as Dresden for its opera house to be rebuilt after wartime destruction. The new house was opened in 1960 and, complete with three small stages, is one of the best equipped theatres in Europe. It replaced the Neues Stadttheater which dated from 1867. Its most exciting era was under Gustav Brecher between 1923 and 1933 when premières of controversial modern works included *Jonny spielt auf* (Johnny strikes up, 1927) by Ernst Křenek (b. 1900), a composer greatly influenced by jazz and cabaret, as was his contemporary Kurt Weill. Weill's updated version of Gay's *Beggar's Opera*, *Die Dreigroschenoper* (The Threepenny Opera), with words by Bertholt Brecht, was a sensation at its first performance in Berlin in 1928. Two years later the première of another of Weill's bitingly satirical works *Aufstieg und Fall der Stadt Mahagonny* (The Rise and Fall of the City of Mahagonny) in Leipzig, caused one of the worst scandals in German theatrical history; rioting spread into the streets and the police were called in to clear the opera house.

BAYREUTH

The five week summer festival in Bayreuth is synonomous with Wagner. Looking for 'a beautiful oasis, far from the smoke and industrial stench of our urban civilisation', Wagner originally chose this small Bavarian town for his cherished dream of a festival

Kurt Weill's The Threepenny Opera *produced by the English Music Theatre in 1976*

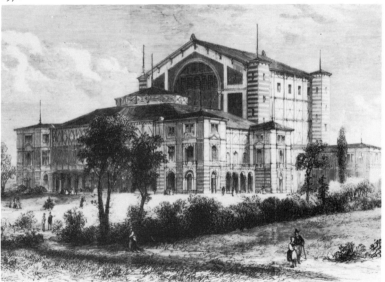

Festspielhaus *at Bayreuth as it appeared for first performance of Wagner's* Ring *in 1876*

devoted to his *Ring* cycle because the opera house, dating from 1748, had the largest stage in Germany. It was one of the few baroque theatres to escape destruction in the Second World War and is still occasionally used for performances today.

Wagner decided he could achieve complete artistic independence only by building his own theatre, and there it stands on a green hill overlooking the town. The auditorium is shaped like a Greek ampitheatre and the pit is sunk below the level of the stage so that the conductor and orchestra are not seen by the audience. Once the plain grey curtains part, there is nothing to distract the audience from the action on stage and sight-lines are excellent from almost all seats in the house. Until Wagner's day, the house lights remained up during an opera performance so that the audience could admire each other's clothes as well as the costumes on stage, but at Bayreuth, before the orchestral prelude begins, the house is always in complete darkness. Wagner designed his theatre very carefully to get the best balance between voices and orchestra; the auditorium has a bare wooden floor and wooden seats, thus producing a very long reverberation time and a distinctive sound quality which is unmistakable in a recording or broadcast.

In 1876 the theatre was completed for the first festival performance of *The Ring* and saved from future financial disaster by the generosity of King Ludwig II. Wagner had already rehearsed the artists the previous summer and the hallmark of the whole enterprise was the total dedication of all concerned and their willingness to submit to long and intensive preparation; this was in contrast to the common practice of prima donnas who sent their maids to dictate where they would stand in performances!

After Wagner's death in 1883, there was a fear that the festivals would lapse, but his widow Cosima emerged from seclusion in the family home, Wahnfried, and remained festival director until 1906; Felix Mottl was her chief producer and Hermann Levi, despite the disadvantage of being a Jew, was the favoured conductor. She became so preoccupied with preserving the absolute authenticity of Wagner's own productions that the death of her father Liszt, from a chill caught at the 1886 festival, went almost unnoticed. Everything on stage was conceived in ultra-realistic terms; under Cosima, Bayreuth petrified, tradition being enshrined with the same rigidity as the D'Oyly Carte's productions of Gilbert and Sullivan.

Although Cosima relinquished her position to her son Seigfried, a prolific though now forgotten opera composer, her influence predominated certainly until 1914. When the festival reopened ten years later, Siegfried was at last able to modernise the lighting equipment and replace the original painted flats with three-dimensional scenery. Singers who made their names at Bayreuth in the 1920s included Friedrich Schorr, Frida Leider, Nanny Larsen-Todsen and Lauritz Melchoir – perhaps it is the Viking physique that makes Scandinavians such good Wagnerian singers! Toscanini was the first non-German conductor to be invited to Bayreuth and gave outstanding performances of *Tristan* and *Tannhäuser* in 1930 and *Parsifal* the following year. He refused, however, to conduct a new production of *Die Meistersinger* in 1933 when Hitler attended the festival in an official capacity. Richard Strauss took over and *Die Meistersinger* was adopted as the national opera of the Third Reich.

Siegfried had married a young English girl who became a close friend of Hitler and even provided him with the paper to write the first volume of *Mein Kampf* when he was imprisoned in Munich. After Siegfried's death in 1930, Winnifred was his heir and became festival director; the official position of Wagner as Hitler's favourite composer and Bayreuth as the symbol of the pure spirit of Aryan German nationalist culture was recognised. The festival was made exempt from taxation and Hitler donated 50,000 marks a year to it from his own pocket.

Winnifred appointed Heinz Tietjen, general administrator of Prussian state theatres, as Bayreuth administrator and Emil Preetorius as designer. Bayreuth became a summer adjunct to the Berlin State Opera, using singers like Rudolf Bockelmann, Margarete Close and Herbert Janssen; it was a useful arrangement as international artists became increasingly unwilling to participate. Kirsten Flagstadt for example found that Americans did not like the fact that she had sung in the 1933 and 1934 Bayreuth Festivals because of their identification with National Socialism and rabid anti-Semitism. During the war the festivals continued as a great Nazi morale booster with special performances of *Die Meistersinger* for factory workers and soldiers.

Because of Bayreuth's political significance, the festival was not resumed until 1951 when revolutionary productions of *Parsifal* and *The Ring* were produced by Wagner's grandson Wieland, with his brother Wolfgang in charge of administration. The new spirit of Bayreuth was expressed by their quotation from Wagner's essay *Art and Revolution*: 'the work of art of the future is intended to express the spirit of free people irrespective of all national boundaries.' Wieland focused attention on Wagner's music by creating simple, stylised productions with subtle lighting effects to suggest supernatural elements, although some people complained they could not see who was singing through the general gloom. He was greatly influenced by the ideas of Adolphe Appia expressed in his book *Productions of Wagner's Dramas* (1895) which his grandmother had found abhorrent when it was published. A new generation of great Wagnerian singers emerged, led by Birgit Nilsson, Wolfgang Windgassen and Hans Hotter under conductors such as Herbert von Karajan and Hans Knappertsbusch.

Since Wieland Wagner's tragically early death in 1966, the double burden of artistic and administrative direction has fallen on his brother. Controversial new productions by guest producers have included Patrice Chéreau's *Ring*, Götz Friedrich's *Tannhäuser* and, another East German, Harry Kupfer's *Flying Dutchman*. Conductors who have made their mark include Pierre Boulez, Colin Davis and Mark Elder, the new young musical director of the English National Opera.

Great Britain

THE ROYAL OPERA HOUSE, COVENT GARDEN
Since the Covent Garden fruit and vegetable market has been moved to Nine Elms in South London, the classical lines of Edward Barry's Royal Opera House, opened in 1858, can be seen to much better advantage. The first theatre built on the site was opened in 1732 by John Rich with the profits from *The Beggar's Opera* , which was naturally his first choice for a musical work in what was primarily a playhouse. Handel's opera company played there for three seasons and was followed by a succession of popular ballad operas. Before the days of electric lighting most theatres burnt down at least once during their history; the second Covent Garden theatre was opened in 1809 under the management of the famous Kemble family of actor-managers with Henry Bishop as musical director. As well as his own works, Bishop adapted

foreign operas for the English stage, including *The Libertine*, his version of Mozart's *Don Giovanni*. He was replaced in 1826 by Carl Maria von Weber, commissioned to write *Oberon* for the sum of £500. Weber died three months after his arrival in England and the next opera of international importance to be commissioned by Covent Garden was Benjamin Britten's *Billy Budd* (1951) 125 years later.

Italian operas proved far more popular than German ones and Maria Malibran was a favourite singer. Throughout the nineteenth century Covent Garden was a house in which one soprano was idolised above all others by the public. For a brief period a British contralto, Lucia Elizabeth Vestris and her husband established a resident British company, a recurrent event in the house's history, but by 1843 their financial situation was so poor that the theatre was leased as a lecture hall to the Anti-Corn Law League; in the First World War it served as a furniture repository and in the Second World War it was a dance hall.

In 1847 it was reopened as the Royal Italian Opera House by a group of defectors from Benjamin Lumley's Italian Company at Her Majesty's Theatre; they included the conductor Michael Costa, the sopranos Persiani and Grisi, Grisi's tenor husband Mario, the contralto Marietta Alboni and the baritone Tamburini. They were joined by Malibran's sister Pauline Viardot-Garcia for a production of Meyerbeer's *Les Huguenots*, the first royal command performance before Queen Victoria in 1848.

Eight years later the building went up in flames after a fancy dress ball. Under the management of Frederick Gye between 1851 and 1877, the Royal Italian Opera House was rebuilt and opened in 1858 with *Les Huguenots* in Italian, the language into which all new works were quickly translated, including Wagner and Gounod. During the winters of 1858 to 1864 it became the Royal English Opera House with all works translated into English; this was due to the enterprise of two English singers, Louisa Fanny Pyne and William Harrison. The three most popular English operas in their repertoire were by two Irishmen and a naturalised German: Michael Balfe's (1808–70) *The Bohemian Girl* (1843), Vincent Wallace's (1812–65) *Maritana* and Julius Benedict's (1804–85) *The Lily of Killarney* (1862).

The reigning queen of the Italian season was Adelina Patti (1843–1919) who sang there every year from 1861 to 1884. She

Mario, Grisi and Alboni in 1847 production of Donizetti's Lucrezia Borgia *at Covent Garden.*

specialised in Rossini, Donizetti and Bellini heroines but later in her career became more dramatic and was the first Covent Garden Aida in 1876. Her fees were phenomenal and her contract stipulated that she was excused rehearsals. When Patti sang the

Covent Garden audience stopped talking, but for the rest of the time they treated performances like a large informal party, eating, drinking and card-playing in the ante-rooms and wandering in and out of the auditorium which remained fully lit, a practice not abandoned until the 1890s.

The only thing that Augustus Harris dimmed while he was manager from 1888 until his early death in 1894 was the lights. His grandfather Joseph Glossop had been the impressario of San Carlo and La Scala in the 1820s and his father was stage manager (the nearest thing to a producer) at Covent Garden. He discontinued the obligatory translation of every opera into Italian, and in 1892, the year Mahler conducted a complete *Ring* cycle in German, the theatre became the Royal Opera House.

Harris assembled a brilliant group of star singers led by Jean de Reszke, Lilian Nordica and Minnie Hauk in sumptuous new stagings fully deserving the title of grand opera. In the face of adverse press criticism he bought *The Sunday Times*; he was already supported by Cornetto di Basso, alias George Bernard Shaw, writing in *The Star*. The Prince and Princess of Wales were patrons of the glittering operatic social scene which was ruled by Lady de Grey. She insisted that Nellie Melba (1861–1931), then an unknown young soprano from Australia, should be re-engaged for the 1889 season to sing Gounod's Juliette. After Harris's death Lady de Grey and Melba wielded immense power and ensured that no rival soprano poached on her favourite roles. Melba's was a voice of almost boy-like purity and despite her later matronly figure she continued to sing 17-year-old Marguerite in *Faust* and Mimi in *La Bohème* until her farewell programme in 1926.

In the first decade of this century, Melba and Caruso dominated an era of superb singing which included the voices of John McCormack, Luisa Tetrazzini, Emmy Destinn and Antonio Scotti; the cosmopolitan status of Covent Garden was emphasised by performances with every leading Italian and German conductor except Toscanini. It was, however, a young English conductor Mr (later Sir) Thomas Beecham who created the greatest stir with a short season in 1910 which included Strauss's *Elektra* and two works by English composers whom he fervently championed: *The Wreckers* by Ethyl Smyth (1858–1944) and *A Village Romeo and Juliet* by Frederick Delius (1862–1934). Dame Ethyl Smyth as she later became was a formidable pioneer woman composer who trained in Leipzig, where Delius, born in Bradford of German descent, also studied for a time. Delius spent most of his life in France, after an early episode on a Florida orange plantation. His other operas were *Koanga* which Beecham conducted at Covent Garden in 1935, *Irmelin*, produced in Oxford in 1953 and *Fennimore and Gerda* (Frankfurt 1919).

Beecham clashed with the censors when he produced Strauss's *Salome* later in 1910, and also in 1913, because of the bed in Act I of *Der Rosenkavalier*. In 1915 he formed his own opera company and after the First World War staged two seasons at Covent Garden, of which he was leaseholder for a short time before financial disaster temporarily ended his career as operatic impressario and conductor. Brief seasons of opera in English were given by the British National Opera Company, conducted by Percy Pitt and Albert Coates, and the Carl Rosa Company which introduced a young Lancashire soprano, Eva Turner, who was later to sing Turandot at La Scala.

The public's need for a grand international season was fulfilled by Bruno Walter who, as artistic director from 1924, specialised in Wagner and Strauss with the Vienna-based quartet of singers Lotte Lehmann, Elisabeth Schumann, Maria Olczewska and Richard Mayr; their *Rosenkavalier* is still nostalgically considered the best that ever was. In 1933 Beecham returned and despite the rise of Hitler and the increasing number of refugees singing at Covent Garden, developed a reciprocal relationship with Furtwängler who came to conduct the Covent Garden *Ring* cycles in 1937 and 1938 while Beecham conducted *Orfeo ed Euridice* in Berlin. Other highlights included Conchita Supervia in Rossini's *La Cenerentola* and Richard Tauber in *The Magic Flute*. English singers who established themselves during the short English seasons organised by the Imperial League of Opera included Tom Burke, Walter Widdop, Dennis Noble and Joan Cross, who was lured away from Sadler's Wells to sing Desdemona opposite Lauritz Melchior's Otello in 1934.

At the end of the Second World War there was a strong possibility that the Royal Opera House would continue to be used as a dance hall but the music publishers Boosey and Hawkes took up the lease until the Covent Garden Opera Trust was formed to run the theatre with the Arts Council. It was to be a national centre of opera performed in English and giving preference to English artists wherever possible, but the best candidate for musical director was Carl Rankl, originally from Austria. David Webster was appointed general administrator, and was succeeded in 1970 by John Tooley. A thousand singers were auditioned throughout the country and an excellent chorus was formed thanks to the long established choral tradition in Wales and the north of England. Soloists of the right calibre were more difficult to find. Eva Turner and Edith Coates who had both been with Beecham in 1939 were an obvious choice but many of the productions had a polyglot cast singing English with a variety of unconvincing accents; for the first *Ring* in 1948 both Kirsten Flagstad and Hans Hotter relearnt their enormously long and taxing roles as no English singers were considered suitable to sing Brünnhilde and Wotan.

The first production by the company was Purcell's *The Fairy Queen* in a new realisation by Constant Lambert (1905–51); the great triumph was 14 performances of *Peter Grimes* with Joan Cross and Peter Pears in the roles they had created at Sadler's Wells. Joan Cross also produced *Rosenkavalier*, having the interest of the music far more at heart than much of the work of the controversial director of productions Peter Brook, and created the role of Elizabeth I in *Gloriana*, the opera commissioned from Benjamin Britten for the coronation of Queen Elizabeth II in 1953. Other operas which have had their world premières at Covent Garden include Sir William Walton's (b. 1902) *Troilus and Cressida* (1954); Sir Michael Tippett's (b. 1905) *The Midsummer Marriage* (1955), (*King Priam* was premièred at the Coventry Festival in 1962) and *The Knot Garden* (1970); Peter Maxwell Davies' (b. 1934) *Taverner* (1972) and John Tavener's (b. 1944) *Thérèse* (1980).

The emergence of British singers of outstanding talent like Amy Shuard, Joan Carlyle, Sylvia Fisher, Monica Sinclair, Michael Langdon and Geraint Evans confirmed the resolution of Rafael Kubelik, the Czech musical director from 1955 to 1958, to implement the opera in English policy. That policy was fully justified by the triumph of the production of Berlioz's *The Trojans* in 1957, with Jon Vickers. However, for the centenary of the house in 1958 Giulini conducted Visconti's superlative production of *Don Carlos* in Italian. There had also been special guest performances in Italian at higher prices, such as Callas in *Norma* in 1952. The 1959 production of Donizetti's *Lucia di Lammermoor* in Italian, stunningly produced by Franco Zeffirelli, led to Joan Sutherland

Sir Michael Tippett's King Priam *at Covent Garden in 1962*

being invited to La Scala and to international recognition for her as a leading exponent of the forgotten art of florid *bel canto* singing.

When Georg Solti was appointed musical director in 1961 his stated aim was to make Covent Garden the best opera house in the world, with opera sung in the original language by hand-picked casts of internationally recognised guest singers, together with members of the regular company, for a limited number of performances. This was the Italian *stagióne* system rather than the German repertory one. During this period the influence of the producer increased, Visconti providing the opulent settings for *Trovatore* and *Rosenkavalier* and Zeffirelli those for *Don Giovanni*, *Rigoletto* and *Tosca*, the latter being Callas's last and perhaps greatest role in the house. Peter Hall established himself in the international league with *Moses and Aaron*, designed by John Bury, in 1965. Among British singers who came to prominence during the 1960s were Gwyneth Jones, Josephine Veasey, Peter Glossop and Stuart Burrows.

The success and recognition of such British singers abroad has totally changed the situation at Covent Garden. There is no longer the need to import an entire foreign ensemble, and since 1971 the Royal Opera has had a British musical director, Colin Davis. New male singing stars include Thomas Allen, Robert Lloyd and Gwynne Howell, and sopranos like Margaret Price and New Zealand-born Kiri te Kanawa have proved worthy partners to the great tenors of the decade, Luciano Pavarotti and Placido Domingo. Elijah Moshinsky has been responsible for award winning productions of *Peter Grimes*, *Lohengrin* and *The Rake's Progress*; a new *Ring* directed by the East German Joachim Herz was more controversial because of its staging but not its musical standards – the Royal Opera House Orchestra is certainly without rivals.

The recognition and achievements of British artists in the international operatic sphere removed the necessity for opera to be performed in English by second-best artists. The disadvantage of Covent Garden's status on a par with La Scala, Vienna and the Met is that the ordinary public who would enjoy opera in the original language are unable to afford it. The enormous costs involved in opera production and the relatively low subsidies compared with West Germany have resulted in far higher ticket prices than in any other London theatre. The image of opera as a luxury entertainment available only to the rich is unfortunately perpetuated at Covent Garden.

ENGLISH NATIONAL OPERA
In 1981 the English National Opera at the London Coliseum celebrated its Golden Jubilee as a company whose aims are 'performing in English, fostering British artists and technicians,

commissioning new works and expanding educational activities so as to introduce more and more new people into the world of opera.'

Its history goes back to a disreputable music hall in Waterloo Road, London, originally the Coburg Theatre of 1816, which was reopened in 1880 by the philanthropist Emma Cons to provide improving entertainment for the working classes with no intoxicating liquor on the premises. In 1898 she brought in her niece Lilian Baylis (1874–1937) to manage the 'Old Vic', as it was to become. Being without a dramatic licence, Lilian Bayliss started introducing operatic excerpts and these developed into regular performances of opera twice a week. Her musical director was Charles Corri whose family trio of piano, violin and 'cello was expanded to an orchestra of 28 for his rescored version of *Tristan and Isolde* which he reduced to three hours running time, including intervals.

Just before the First World War, Lilian Baylis also founded the Old Vic Shakespeare Company led by Sybil Thorndike. When Sir Thomas Beecham went bankrupt at Covent Garden in 1920, she was left to provide London with its major supply of opera throughout the year. Verdi, Donizetti and Mozart, in excellent new translations by E. J. Dent, were all in the repertoire along with *Carmen, Cav* and *Pag* (*Cavalleria Rusticana* and *I Pagliacci*), *Tannhäuser, Lohengrin* and British operas like Ethyl Smyth's *The Boatswain's Mate* and Nicholas Gatty's *The Tempest*.

It was a remarkable personal achievement in the face of overwhelming odds, and showed that opera well sung and simply presented did appeal to ordinary working people who could only afford to pay sixpence for a seat in the gallery, where they all felt part of her family. 'The Lady', as she was affectionately known, was a battle-axe of extraordinary personal magnetism who could persuade artists to sing for no pay, or £3 a week, convincing them that it was a privilege to 'help the Vic'. Her regular singers included Joan Cross, Edith Coates and Heddle Nash. Her chorus were amateurs trained by Lawrence Collingwood in a disused pub after working hours and for performances, for which they were paid two shillings and sixpence, they wore one of three standard costumes: all-purpose peasant for *Carmen*, a tabard for anything German, and lace with a shawl for Mozart!

In 1931 she opened another derelict theatre, Sadler's Wells in

Islington, to be an Old Vic for North London. It had been built in 1683 by a certain Dick Sadler as a 'Musick-house' for the patrons of his medicinal wells. From 1934 the rebuilt theatre was taken over by the permanent opera company and the newly founded Vic-Wells Ballet, while the Old Vic was given to the Shakespeare

Lilian Bayliss (1874–1937)

Company. The policy of opera in English was vindicated by the immediacy of the audience's response; when John Christie, Glyndebourne's founder, went to hear his wife Audrey Mildmay sing Susanna at Sadler's Wells, he was astonished to hear the audience laugh at the jokes in the libretto! Other guest artists included Maggie Teyte, Florence Austral and Astra Desmond; Adrian Boult conducted *Don Giovanni* playing the recitatives at the piano and John Barbirolli conducted *The Barber of Seville*. The resident conductors were Lawrence Collingwood and Warwick Braithwaite and the small nucleus of regular singers who found themselves singing an enormous number of roles with very little preparation included Joan Cross, Edith Coates, Janet Hamilton-Smith, Tudor Davies, Redvers Llewllyn, John Hargeaves and Ronald Stear. Powell Lloyd and Sumner Austin had to double as producers and designers as well as sing. The company's teamwork spirit produced a freshness and standard of ensemble performance in productions of *Falstaff* and *Boris Godunov* which impressed even Toscanini.

Modern British opera was championed with performances of Gustav Holst's (1874–1934) *Sávitri*, Sir Charles Villiers Stanford's (1852–1924) *The Travelling Companion*, and Ralph Vaughan Williams' (1872–1958) *Hugh the Drover*. Miss Baylis would berate her audiences in her famous first night speeches: 'You'd better come to these ones, even if you don't like them, else we won't be able to afford the ones you do like!'

Tyrone Guthrie was appointed director of the Old Vic and Sadler's Wells companies after her sudden death in 1937. Two years later war broke out and Sadler's Wells became a touring company and enormously increased the popularity of opera throughout the country under the leadership of Joan Cross as company manager.

The theatre reopened in June 1945 with the world première of Benjamin Britten's *Peter Grimes*; the cast was led by Joan Cross and Peter Pears and conducted by Reginald Goodall. For the first time since Purcell's *Dido and Aeneas*, a British composer was firmly established with a masterpiece of international acceptability. Sadler's Wells was hard hit by the decision of the new Covent Garden company to present opera in English and the transformation of the Sadler's Wells ballet company into the Royal Ballet, also based at Covent Garden. Under Norman Tucker, director from 1951 to 1966, it was decided to concentrate in their smaller theatre on a more unusual repertoire, winning them a reputation for excellence in widely differing fields. Alexander Gibson as musical director, and later Colin Davis, presented lesser known comic operas by Rossini, forgotten Verdi and operetta, particularly Offenbach's *Orpheus in the Underworld*, in sparkling new translations and productions. Janáček's operas became another speciality starting with Denis Arundel's production of *Kátya Kabanová* in 1951 and continuing under the baton of Charles Mackerras whose definitive interpretation of the scores dates from his studies in Prague.

Commitment to modern opera remained high, aiming at one new production a year and included John Gardner's *The Moon and Sixpence* (1957), Lennox Berkeley's *Nelson* (1953), Richard Rodney Bennett's *The Mines of Sulphur* (1965), and Malcolm Williamson's *Our Man in Havanna* (1963) and *The Violins of St Jacques* (1966). To cope with the expanded repertoire new singers were acquired, many from Australia, while retaining a closely knit company of regulars. Among those associated with Sadler's Wells who went on to make international careers were Amy Shuard, Patricia Johnson, Charles Craig, David Ward, Donald McIntyre, Peter Glossop and more recently Rita Hunter, Alberto Remedios and Norman Bailey. Productions were in the hands of a regular team of specialists like Anthony Besch, Wendy Toye, Basil Coleman and the new talent of Colin Graham and John Blatchley, as well as straight theatre directors such as George Devine, Frank Hauser and Peter Hall.

When the project to build a new opera house adjacent to the National Theatre on the South Bank of the Thames fell through, Stephen Arlen, managing director from 1966, set his sights on London's largest theatre, the Coliseum, a stone's throw from Trafalgar Square. Built at the beginning of the century by Sir Oswald Stoll, its distinguished past included performances by Sarah Bernhardt and the Diaghilev ballet before housing the lavish British premières of American musicals like *Kiss me, Kate* and *Guys and Dolls*.

The original company spirit of ensemble productions rather than using stars has been maintained, no longer with an excuse for lower standards because of cramped stage and orchestra space. Under the musical directorship of Charles Mackerras from 1970 to 1978, orchestral standards were greatly improved. One of the greatest achievements made possible by the increased size of its new home was a complete *Ring* cycle in English, conducted by Reginald Goodall and produced by Glen Byam Shaw and John Blatchley. In 1974 a change of status was recognised by a new name, The English National Opera, under the directorship of Lord Harewood.

The policy of promoting modern opera has continued and commissioned works have included Ian Hamilton's *The Royal Hunt of the Sun* (1977) and *Anna Karenina* for the jubilee season in 1981. The English National goes into the 1980s with its youngest ever musical director, Mark Elder, who made his Bayreuth debut in 1981 and was joined in 1982 by David Pountney from Scottish Opera as director of productions.

Widening the repertoire to include grand opera classics like *Aida* and *Arabella* has led to a much looser distinction between artists who are permanently with the company and those who are regular guests. Janet Baker is amongst the most distinguished of these, making possible outstanding productions like *Werther* (1977) and *Julius Caesar* (1979). Artists such as Valerie Masterson, Josephine Barstow, Elizabeth Connell, John Brecknock and John Tomlinson have launched major international careers while still regarding the English National as their home company for much of the year.

The development of other successful opera companies in Britain in recent years has meant that British singers can now look outside London for prestigious engagements. The Welsh National, Scottish Opera, Kent Opera and the English National's own sibling company based in Leeds, now established as the independent Opera North, all have excellent touring productions to cater for opera's ever growing audience.

THE ALDEBURGH FESTIVAL

Benjamin Britten (1913–76) succeeded in establishing Britain on the international operatic map for the first time since the days of Handel. After the success of *Peter Grimes* he formed, with designer John Piper and librettist Eric Crozier, the English Opera Group based in Aldeburgh, the small Suffolk fishing town in which the opera is set. Here Britten and Peter Pears, for whom Grimes and the leading tenor roles in his subsequent operas were written, lived for many years. In 1947 the Aldeburgh Festival was founded to be a focal centre for his works. Over the years it became a unique mixture of international musicians (Visnevskaya and Rostropovitch were favourite visitors) local people and the young singers who formed the company to perform his chamber operas, specially written for the cramped space of the Jubilee Hall. Local children joined in for his two children's operas *Let's Make An Opera* (1949) and *Noye's Fludde* (1958).

The English Opera Group travelled widely abroad, *The Turn of the Screw* for example received its première in Venice (1954). The Aldeburgh success of the chamber opera version of *A Midsummer Night's Dream* (1960) highlighted the need for a larger auditorium. In 1967 the converted Maltings in the neighbouring village of Snape was opened as a beautiful concert hall, but it had to be rebuilt after fire destroyed it. Meanwhile Britten exploited the wonderful setting of the mediaeval churches of Orford and Blyburgh for his church parables: *Curlew River* (1964), *The Burning Fiery Furnace* (1966) and *The Prodigal Son* (1968). His final opera was *Death in Venice* (1973) based on the story by Thomas Mann.

GLYNDEBOURNE

Taking the train from London's Victoria Station in the middle of the afternoon in full evening dress gives one a hint that Glyndebourne is quite unlike any other opera house. Wandering round the old manor house set in the lush green Sussex Downs, or consuming one's picnic hamper by the lake or in the walled gardens during the long supper interval, it seems more a private house party than a commercial venture. The spirit of Captain John Christie, the best kind of English eccentric, still imbues the whole enterprise. Inspired by visits to Salzburg and his marriage to Audrey Mildmay, a young soprano from the Carl Rosa Opera Company, he decided to build his own small opera house in 1934 as the centre for a Mozart festival. The Nazi's rise to power in Germany enabled him to secure the services of Fritz Busch (Dresden) as musical director, Carl Ebert (Berlin) as chief producer and Rudolph Bing (Vienna) as general manager. Together they achieved a standard of perfection which has rarely been equalled in productions of *Figaro*, *Così fan tutte*, *Don Giovanni*, *Entführung* and *Die Zauberflöte*, as well as Verdi's *Macbeth* and Donizetti's *Don Pasquale*.

Glyndebourne reopened after the Second World War with the

première of Benjamin Britten's *The Rape of Lucretia* in 1946 with a cast including Kathleen Ferrier, Joan Cross, Peter Pears and Otakar Kraus. Among the first artists to be persuaded to spend the summer in Glyndebourne's idyllic surroundings were Eric Kunz, Sena Jurinac and George London. The festival developed a reputation for introducing young artists to Britain at the beginning of their international careers as well as fostering British singers. One wing of the house is provided for producers, conductors and junior music staff and other artists enjoy the peaceful atmosphere of country cottages or digs in neighbouring Lewes. However, rigorous working discipline is imposed. Total commitment is expected from all artists for a month's rehearsals before each production with a five-and-a-half-day rehearsal week, including Saturdays and Sundays. There is a far less generous granting of N.A.s (not available) for other engagements during this period

Valerie Masterson in Glyndebourne production of Mozart's Die Entführung aus dem Serail *(1980)*

than is the custom with other companies. There is no star system and the level of fees is not very high. Artists used to complain about the meticulous musical standards and endless rehearsals demanded by the late Jani Strasser, the veteran head of music staff, but the final result always justified the enormous dedication and hard work involved.

Another outstanding feature of the Glyndebourne system is the excellence of the chorus, usually solo singers who accept a chorus contract because they often cover (understudy) principal roles in the main season and then have the chance of singing them with the touring company in the autumn. British singers who have risen from the Glyndebourne ranks to stardom recently include Anne Howells, Elizabeth Gale, Rosalind Plowright, Sarah Walker, Ryland Davies, Stafford Dean and Richard van Allan.

Glyndebourne remains true to the aims of its founders by providing 'the superb performance, assisted by a marvellous holiday *Festspiel* atmosphere', but over the years the personnel has changed. In 1949 when Rudolph Bing left to run the Edinburgh Festival and later the New York Metropolitan, he was succeeded as general manager by Moran Caplat; when Busch died in 1951, Vittorio Gui became chief conductor, followed in turn by John Pritchard and since 1978 by Bernard Haitinck. In 1959 George Christie took over from his father as chairman of the Glyndebourne Festival Opera.

Although Mozart remains the core of the repertoire – the 1970s saw an excellent new series of productions by Peter Hall of the National Theatre – it has been widened considerably to include Stravinsky's *The Rake's Progress* and the première of Hans Werner Henze's opera *Elegy for Young Lovers* in 1961. Vittorio Gui instigated a brilliant series of Rossini and Donizetti comic operas; another landmark was Raymond Leppard's realisation of Monteverdi's *L'Incoronazione di Poppea* in 1963 which started the revival of baroque opera that subsequently swept Western Europe and America. Leppard then introduced Cavalli's *L'Ormindo* and *La Calisto*; the latter was a marvellous triumph for Janet Baker in the leading role, as was Monteverdi's *Il Ritorno d'Ulisse in Patria* in which she was partnered by Benjamin Luxon. Luxon is another British star who has developed his versatility in Glyndebourne productions of Janáček's *The Cunning Little Vixen* and Mozart's *Don Giovanni*.

Italy

LA SCALA

Italy, the original home of opera in the seventeenth century, remains today the greatest nation of opera lovers, the most vociferous in support of artists and works they love and the most deafeningly damning of those they dislike. It also has some of the world's most famous opera houses, foremost among them being La Scala in Milan.

The original building was opened in 1778 on the site of a demolished church, Santa Maria alla Scala; it had no connection with stairs or ladders, but was named after the wife of one of the Visconti, the great ruling family who were always patrons of the arts and are best known in recent years for the outstanding producer Luchino Visconti (1906–76). Gluck turned down the commission to write the opening opera which came instead from Mozart's rival Salieri.

Despite being completely rebuilt after destruction in an air raid in 1943, La Scala today looks very much as it did 200 years ago, a solid brick building whose yellow and white exterior blends comfortably into the centre of Italy's largest industrial and commercial city. Inside all is dignity and magnificence, in red, gold and white, with four tiers of boxes and two galleries rising round the stalls to seat 3,600 spectators. Gaming tables are no longer allowed inside the theatre though they were a valuable source of revenue when it was first opened and the only gambling in the city allowed by the police; the police also excluded dogs from all parts of the building and strictly forbade the audience to express their disapproval of artists or to ask for encores. The no encore rule is still in force and when La Scala's greatest conductor Arturo Toscanini (1867–1957) was conducting *Un ballo in Maschera* in 1903 he would not give way to audience demands for an encore from tenor Zenatello, threw his baton at the mob, walked off the rostrum and refused to return to the theatre for the next three years.

Rossini, Bellini and Donizetti all enjoyed some of their greatest successes at La Scala. When *La Pietra del Paragone* (The Touchstone) ran for 53 performances in 1812, Rossini was rewarded by the French commander in Milan by exemption from military service – the story that a love-lorn countess intrigued on his behalf is mythical. Not so the lady who failed to gain Bellini's affections – she hired a hostile *claque* who ruined the first performance of *Norma* in 1831, but her money did not cover the second night which was a deserved triumph. The defiant chorus 'Guerra, guerra' (To war, to war) was taken up by the Milanese to express their resentment against their Austrian overlords in the same way that Verdi's choruses from *Nabucco* and *I Lombardi* became great cries of Italian nationalism. 'Va pensiero sull'ali dorati' (Go, thought, on golden wings), a paraphrase of one of his favourite psalms, caught Verdi's eye and persuaded him to write *Nabucco* for impresario Bartolomeo Merelli after the tragic death of his wife and children. Sixty years later Toscanini conducted this chorus at Verdi's funeral, and then at the reopening of La Scala in 1946; it was sung in turn when Toscanini's body was sent home from New York for burial in Milan.

Toscanini started his career as an orchestral 'cellist and played in the La Scala pit for the first performance of Verdi's *Otello* in 1887. In 1898 he took over musical control of the theatre, with Giulio Gatti-Casazza as director general, and started a five-year war with La Scala audiences over artistic standards. His battles with singers were equally vehement, culminating in his fight with Caruso who wanted to rehearse *La Bohème* singing mezza voce (half voice). Their quarrels turned Caruso's long-awaited debut at La Scala into a disappointing failure but he quickly redeemed himself in Donizetti's *L'Elisir d'Amore* and brought the house down with 'Una furtiva lagrima' (Who can deceive a loving heart).

Cleofonte Campanini succeeded Toscanini and conducted the première of Puccini's opera *Madama Butterfly* in 1904. A large anti-Puccini faction succeeded in wrecking the performance and the opera was not performed again at La Scala as long as the composer lived. Toscanini conducted a posthumous première of Puccini's last unfinished opera *Turandot* in 1926 and laid down his baton at the point where Puccini had stopped writing, when the slave girl Liu's body is taken off stage. The opera was complete by Alfano.

Giacomo Puccini (1858–1924) was one of the new *verismo* or realistic Italian opera composers, following the then current trend of naturalism in literature combined with an interest in social problems which was typified by the novels of Emile Zola. They were also reacting against the romantic ideals of Wagner and Verdi. Instead of history and mythology they took their scenes and

Arturo Toscanini (1867–1957)

Puccini's Madama Butterfly *at Covent Garden (1971)*

characters from everyday life and used vivid melodramatic plots. Puccini's first opera *Le Villi* (The Witches) was first performed in 1884 at a smaller Milan theatre, the Teatro dal Verme, where Toscanini, in 1892, conducted the première of *I Pagliacci* (The Strolling Players) by Ruggiero Leoncavallo (1858–1919). The latter opera was based on a true incident at Montalto in Calabria (Southern Italy) where an actor in a touring company murdered his wife; Leoncavallo's father was the judge at the trial. Leoncavallo never equalled its success and since its earliest days the opera has been inextricably joined in a double bill with another short masterpiece *Cavalleria Rusticana* (Rustic Chivalry) by Pietro Mascagni (1863–1945). This won first prize in a competition organised by the music publisher Sonzogno and made the young composer famous overnight when it was produced in Rome in 1890. None of his dozen later operas approached the success of this one.

In contrast Puccini, who developed a marvellous facility for writing arias which were a succession of melodic high points, produced four other masterpieces as well as his triple bill of one act operas: *Manon Lescaut* (Turin 1893), *La Bohème* (Turin 1896), *Tosca* (Rome 1900) and *La Fanciulla del West* (The Girl of the Golden

West, New York 1910). Two other *verismo* works which have retained their popularity are *Andrea Chénier* (Milan 1896) by Umberto Giordano (1867–1948) and *Adriana Lecouvreur* (1902) by Francesco Cilea (1866–1950). The only German equivalent in naturalistic opera to survive is *Tiefland* (The Lowland, Prague 1903) by Eugen d'Albert (1864–1932) who was born in Newcastle on Tyne and brought up in Glasgow!

The two Puccini premières in New York were due to the fact that both Toscanini and Gatti-Casazza left La Scala for the Metropolitan in 1908. Gatti-Casazza remained there as general manager until 1935 but Toscanini returned to the helm of La Scala in 1921 when it was reorganised as an *ente autonomo* (a self-governing corporation). He combined the roles of administrator, impresario and stage director with that of conductor and took the company on tours to Vienna and Berlin, demonstrating the superb achievement of his artistic integrity. He refused to compromise with Mussolini, the fascist dictator, who wanted his portrait hung in the foyer and the fascist national anthem 'Giovinezza' played before every performance.

Toscanini regretfully left La Scala for the New York Philharmonic Orchestra and never conducted a complete opera performance there again. His last appearance there was in 1948 conducting scenes from Boito's *Mefistofele* and *Nerone* on the thirtieth anniversary of the composer's death. He was greatly saddened by the death of his protégé Guido Cantelli who was killed in an air crash in 1956, a few months after conducting *Così fan tutte* at the Piccola Scala, the small auditorium nestling in the wing of the parent house.

Other great Italian conductors at La Scala have included Tullio Serafin, Victorio Gui, Victor de Sabata and Carlo Maria Giullini, whose all too brief relationship with the theatre from 1952 to 1956 produced the collaboration of Maria Callas and Luchino Visconti in Gluck's *Alceste* and Verdi's *La Traviata* – opera at its thrilling best. The later relationship of Callas with Antonio Ghiringhelli, the industrialist appointed as overall director of La Scala, was a very stormy one and the rivalry between Callas and Renata Tebaldi divided the audience into two irreconcilable factions, each claiming the supremacy of their favoured prima donna. There was a similar rivalry between the two most glamorous tenors of the post-war period, Mario del Monaco and Guiseppe Di Stephano, but contraltos Feodora Barbieri and Guiletta Simionato managed an amicable coexistence.

Paolo Grassi succeeded Ghiringhelli after 26 years of administrative command, and since the untimely death of conductor and composer Bruno Maderna, Claudio Abbado has been chief resident conductor, facing the problems of financial corruption, industrial unrest among musicians and political pressure, apart from artistic exigencies.

La Scala remains the greatest opera house in the world, a magnet for the best known singers, conductors, producers and designers. The current generation of favourite Italian singers who have made their mark there includes sopranos Renata Scotto and Mirella Freni, mezzo Fiorenza Cossotto, tenors Luigi Alva (born in Peru) and Luciano Pavarotti, and baritones and basses Cesare Siepi, Piero Cappuccilli and Ruggiero Raimondi.

The audience at La Scala remains notoriously hard to please but there is no sound to compare with the great purr of pleasure which runs through the house when it decides to take a newcomer to its heart.

LA FENICE, VENICE

La Fenice has been described as the most beautiful theatre in the world. The most glamorous way to approach it is by water, alighting from a gondola to go up the steps of the canal entrance and into the foyer. The great Spanish soprano Maria Malibran (1808–36), one of the Venetians' most fêted singers, hated the funereal black of the gondolas and insisted on having her own decorated in scarlet and gold with blue curtains and her gondolier in livery to match. The Teatro San Giovanni Grisostomo, built in 1678 and the second oldest surviving Venetian theatre, was renamed Teatro Malibran in her honour, but today it languishes as a cinema.

The Fenice, opened in 1792, is the youngest of Venice's theatres, and rose like the phoenix of its name from the ashes of a previous theatre on another site. The design was chosen in an open competition for a theatre that would 'appeal at once to the eye as well as to the ear of the spectator'. The opening production was one of the hundred operas written by Giovanni Paisiello. In 1813 Rossini's *Tancredi* established the tradition of world premières of lasting successes at La Fenice. The gondoliers, who have the privilege of free entry to Venice's theatres, plied their trade singing the most popular aria of the day 'Di tanti palpiti', known as the 'rice aria' since Rossini was supposed to have composed it one evening in four minutes while waiting for the rice to boil! In *Semiramide* (1823) the audience loved the military band he brought on stage so much that they hired bands on gondolas to serenade him home after the performance.

Bellini and Donizetti enjoyed brilliant premières in the Fenice, but before the first performance in Venice of *Lucia di Lammermoor* was due to open the 1836 carnival season, it was burnt down and rebuilt within a year. Donizetti declined the invitation to write a new opera to open the 1844 season, complaining of ill treatment by the management; in his place, Verdi wrote *Ernani* and managed to overcome the objection by the President of the Fenice to a French horn being played on stage! *Ernani*, like *Attila* and *Macbeth*, caused great patriotic demonstrations against the Austrians. While rehearsing *Rigoletto*, which ran into serious trouble with the Austrian censor, Verdi forbade the tenor to sing 'La donna e mobile', wanting to keep its enormous potential popularity secret until the first performance. Two years later in 1853, Verdi was deeply distressed by the unfavourable reception which greeted *La Traviata*; on the opera's centenary in 1953 the Fenice made ample amends for the 'fiasco' of that first night. *Simon Boccanegra* (1857) did not please the first night audience either.

There is some confusion about the next musically significant event in Venice which was simultaneous performances of two versions of *La Bohème*, Toscanini conducting Puccini's version, and the world première of Leoncavallo's version presumed to have been at the Fenice on 6 May 1897. It is not included in the theatre's list of world premières which, since the Second World War, has included Stravinsky's *The Rake's Progress* in 1951, Britten's *The Turn of the Screw* in 1954 and Prokofiev's *The Fiery Angel* in 1955. The theatre was completely modernised in 1936 when it became a self-governing corporation and the box holders relinquished their privileges, 300 years after the world's first public opera house was opened in Venice.

Unlike German provincial houses, the Fenice does not have a year-round repertory season. Since 1970, under the artistic direction of Mario Labroca, a pupil of Respighi and Malapiero, the season has been lengthened from eight weeks to five months, and

Interior of La Fenice in Venice

to 70 performances of 15 operas, plus ballets. Perhaps the most celebrated event at the Fenice in recent years was the transformation in 1949 of Maria Callas from Wagner's Brünnhilde to Elvira in Bellini's *I Puritani* in the space of three days. So began her second career as a brilliant exponent of florid singing and the revival of early nineteenth-century *bel canto* operas. Joan Sutherland, another great exponent of this repertoire, made her Italian debut at the Fenice in Handel's *Alcina*.

SAN CARLO, NAPLES

Il Teatro San Carlo in Naples has a grandeur and elegance all of its own. Built by Charles of Bourbon, later King Charles III of Spain, in 1737 adjoining his royal palace, it was to be a 'new and grandiose' theatre, a fitting home for the lavish productions of serious opera with numerous ballets which he loved, as opposed to the delightful comedies for which eighteenth-century Naples was famous. The auditorium was refulgent with hundreds of candles grouped in front of six tiers of boxes: the higher up the social ladder a person was, the more candles there were in front of his or her box. Fourteen-year-old Mozart, in 1770, described a typical baroque spectacle there, the première of *Armida abbandonata* by Niccolo Jommelli (1714–74), a popular Neapolitan composer:

'The dances are wretchedly pompous. The King ... always stands on a stool so as to look a little taller than the Queen.'

Naples had a large English colony presided over by the ambassador Sir William Hamilton and his wife Lady Hamilton. They patronised the beautiful London soprano Mrs Elizabeth Billington when she arrived in 1794 and insisted that she sing to the King and Queen and then at the San Carlo. Her success there was marred by an eruption of Vesuvius which the superstitious blamed on the engagement of a foreign heretic. Her rival, Guiseppina Grassini, became Napoleon's mistress and eventually director of concerts and theatres at the Imperial French Court. But the most colourful figure in the history of the San Carlo is undoubtedly the 'Prince of Impressarios', Domenico Barbaia, who started his incredible opera house management career in Naples in 1810.

He engaged Rossini to write two operas a year and in addition to a salary of 10,000 francs a year (about £400), gave him a share in the profits of the gambling tables in the theatre and free board and lodging in his house. He later regretted the extent of his generosity when Rossini went off with his mistress, Isabella Colbran; as neither of them could dispense with her services as a singer, for business purposes they remained a harmonious trio, with King Ferdinand I, another previous admirer, making it a quartet.

In 1816 Rossini returned from the première of *The Barber of Seville* in Rome to find that the San Carlo had burnt down, the result of a spark from a lantern left on stage after a ballet rehearsal. It was rebuilt in seven months with an enlarged stage and auditorium and the splendid painted ceiling ('Apollo presenting to Minerva the world's most famous poets from Homer to Alfieri') which remains one of its chief attractions today. Neapolitan audiences have always been famous for their unruliness and according to Stendhal when, at the 1819 première of Rossini's *La Donna del Lago* (based on Scott's poem 'The Lady of the Lake') the tenor sang out of tune, the audience became 'roaring, ravenous lions. ... Nothing can give the least, the sketchiest idea of a Neapolitan audience insulted by a wrong note!'

Barbaia eventually retired from Naples in 1840 having also fostered the careers of Bellini and Donizetti. Verdi's relationship with the San Carlo was a somewhat stormy one. His first commissioned opera *Alzira* was a failure, but *I due Foscari*, performed a few months earlier in 1845, had met with more success due to the singing of an English prima donna, Anna Bishop, wife of Sir Henry, composer of 'Home sweet home'. She had run away with a French composer and harpist and after two years at the San Carlo, wandered the world as far as China and Honolulu, before dying in New York.

For some years Verdi wanted to write an opera based on *King Lear* for the San Carlo, but in face of numerous difficulties he substituted *Gustave III*. He refused to agree with the censor's drastic alterations to the libretto and withdrew the work. The people of Naples were on his side against the management who tried to sue him, and covered the walls with 'Viva Verdi' which also stands for *Viva Vittorio Emanuele Re D'Italia*, expressing Verdi's championship of Italian independence. The opera was eventually produced in Rome as *Un Ballo in Maschera*.

One of the greatest ironies of the San Carlo was the lack of success that Naples' most famous singer found there. In 1901 Enrico Caruso was given a lukewarm reception in *L'Elisir d'Amore* and Massenet's *Manon* and never appeared there again.

In the Mussolini era there were more censorship problems and the première of *L'Aiglon* by Arthur Honegger and Jacques Ibert was suddenly cancelled in 1937, but Honegger's *Judith*, Bloch's *Macbeth* and Kodaly's *The Spinning Room of the Székelys* were all allowed.

In 1943 Allied bombs destroyed the foyer but the theatre was undamaged and when the troops entered Naples, British forces under Brigadier Cripps requisitioned the San Carlo for concerts and operas. Nearly two million British and American servicemen became enthusiasts for Italian grand opera during the next three years. The company included singers of international reputation such as Gigli, Maria Caniglia, Ebe Stignani, Francesco Merli and Toti Dal Monte, as well as new singers like Tito Gobbi, Paolo Silveri, Ferruccio Tagliavini and Luigi Infantino who were destined for stardom. After the war a plaque in the rebuilt foyer commemorated their achievement of 'keeping alive the flame of its traditions and entrusting to the wings of song this message which unites in brotherhood the hearts of the people of all nations.'

When Covent Garden reopened in 1946 it was a company from the San Carlo that gave a two-month opera season there. Without producing any noticeable world premières, the theatre and its repertoire continue to flourish, together with the little court theatre, Teatro di Corte, alongside. This was opened in 1954 for performances of those essentially Neapolitan comic operas by Cimarosa, Pergolesi and Paisiello.

IL TEATRO REGIO, PARMA

The city of Parma has one of Italy's most famous music conservatoires whose students have included Toscanini, Renata Tebaldi, Carlo Bergonzi and the composer Ildebrando Pizzetti (1880–1968) whose best known opera was a setting of T. S. Eliot's *Murder in the Cathedral*. It also has Italy's second oldest theatre, the Farnese, dating from 1628 and built entirely of wood; it has now been rebuilt after partial destruction during the Second World War, but what does one do with a seventeenth-century wooden theatre last used for court performances in 1732?

Parma does have a very attractive and usable opera house, the Teatro Regio which is well worth a visit, even if no opera is being performed there, for the lavish white and gold decorations of the auditorium and the elegantly furnished ante-rooms of the boxes. A unique feature is the dressing rooms for the principals at the side of the stage, cutting out the usual long walk along corridors or up and down stairs before they can relax or change costumes between scenes. Everything about the theatre is in Empire style, appropriately enough, since it was built by Napoleon's second wife, the Empress Marie Louise who declined to accompany him into exile. Instead she reigned as Duchess of Parma until her death in 1847.

The theatre opened in 1829 and has an auditorium modelled on that of La Scala and a magnificent painted ceiling and curtain representing 'The Triumph of Knowledge'. The failure of Bellini's *Zaira* (he was only second choice to Rossini anyway), was a presage of the highly critical standards the Parmigiani have continued to apply to operas and singers. They have always regarded Verdi as their own special property; his birthplace is only 30 miles away but they tend to ignore the fact that the Teatro Regio turned down the opportunity of producing his first opera *Oberto, conte di San Bonifacio* in 1836 because it was considered too great a risk. Parma was the obvious choice for the Institute of Verdi Studies, founded in 1959 under the joint auspices of UNESCO and the Italian Government with Pizzetti as its first president. A favourite cautionary tale of the dangers of singing Verdi in Parma is of the Radames in a 1929 performance of *Aida* who was known to own a bicycle shop in

Milan. In the hushed silence of the final scene in the tomb, a voice from the gods called out, 'You little man, when you've finished, will you come and mend my bicycle?'

Although Toscanini was born in Parma, he never conducted an opera at the Regio. He started his career playing the 'cello in the orchestra pit there, under Cleofonte Campanini (1860–1919), who brought the orchestra to such a pitch of excellence that it was awarded first prize in a competition for opera orchestras. Campanini's brother was the famous tenor Italo Campanini who sang Faust at the opening of the Metropolitan Opera in 1883 and his wife's sister was the great soprano Luisa Tetrazzini (1871–1940). In 1914 he organised a singing competition and amongst the new talent discovered Beniamino Gigli; 'AT LAST WE HAVE FOUND THE TENOR' wrote one of the Jury in capital letters.

Many world famous singers have failed to please on the stage of the Regio. Conchita Supervia was a failure as Carmen in 1924; Tito Gobbi was criticised for the elegance of his car until he proved that his voice was equally superb in his debut as the Barber of Seville in 1946; Emma Carelli, Toscanini's prima donna at La Scala, was so appalled by the audience's treatment of the rest of the cast in Ponchielli's *La Gioconda* in 1903 that she returned their insults and left for the railway station in full costume and make-up. She was obviously a lady of very strong character as she went on to manage the Constanzi theatre in Rome from 1911 to 1925.

Spain

Spain has a strongly developed tradition of light operas named *zarzuela*, after the palace outside Madrid where musical entertainments were performed in the seventeenth century. Tonadillas are short popular operettas lasting 10 to 20 minutes which evolved in the eighteenth century in reaction to the dictatorship of Italian singers and Italian opera. They are based on traditional Spanish songs and dances which vary according to the province from which they come, but all have distinctive rhythms and tonality, often of Moorish and gypsy influence, like the *polo* from Andalusia or the *jota* from Navarre.

In the second half of the nineteenth century there was a nationalistic revival of music and literature in Spain; the Teatro de

Zarzuela was opened in Madrid in 1856 for what became the most popular form of musical entertainment based on stories about ordinary people and containing street songs in which all the audience could join. The *zarzuela grande* is a whole evening's entertainment in three acts and the *genero chico*, which is usually comic, is in one act. The best known composers included Francisco Barbieri (1823–94), Joaquin Gazambide (1822–70) and Tomas Bretón (1850–1923), collaborating with some of the most popular writers of the day.

The *zarzuela* retains its popularity today in Spain and South America. It also influenced the three internationally known Spanish composers: Isaac Albéniz (1860–1909); Enrique Granados (1867–1916) whose ship was torpedoed by a German submarine as he was returning from the New York première of Albéniz's opera *Goyescas*; and Manuel de Falla (1876–1946) whose opera *La Vida Breva* (A Short Life, Nice 1913) makes similar attractive use of Spanish traditional music and is undeservedly neglected.

When Spain's leading opera house, the Teatro del Liceo in Barcelona, was originally built in 1847 it was one of Europe's largest theatres. It suffered the usual fate of being destroyed by fire and the theatre standing today was reopened in 1862. De Falla's opera *Atlantida* was given a posthumous première there in 1961 featuring Victoria de los Angeles, one of the best loved Spanish singers since the Second World War; she made her debut in the house in 1945. Spain has produced other outstanding female singers including Conchita Supervia (1899–1936), and amongst today's international artists are Teresa Berganza and Montserrat Caballé, not forgetting the great tenor Placido Domingo whose parents were *zarzuela* singers in Mexico.

Sweden

Sweden's operatic fame was inaugurated by Gustavus III who founded the Royal Opera in Stockholm and was fatally wounded at a masked ball held in his opera house in 1792. This was the basis for Verdi's *Un Ballo in Maschera* and the most sensational production of the opera was in the present house (opened in 1891) in the 1950s with Ragnar Ulfung portraying an historically correct Gustavus as a high heeled, berouged homosexual, mocked at and murdered by a recalcitrant aristocracy.

After the First World War, Armas Järnfelt, brother-in-law of Sibelius, brought new life and an excellent ensemble of singers to the opera. Together with producer Harald André he collaborated in a brilliant series of avant-garde productions.

Since the days of Jenny Lind (1820–87), Sweden has been renowned for her singers; the problem is that once they achieve international fame they no longer sing regularly in Stockholm. Svet Svanholm (1904–64) who sang all the great Wagnerian tenor roles retired from his singing career to return as general administrator of the Stockholm Opera in the 1950s. Another great Swedish tenor and favourite at the Metropolitan was Jussi Björling; Niccolai Gedda still continues with his remarkable career as do Birgit Nilsson, Elisabeth Söderström and Berit Lindholm.

Some of the most interesting productions in recent years in Stockholm have been under the directorship of Ingmar Bergman who brought a fresh look to the world of opera after his acclaimed career as a film director. His most widely known success has been a delightful film version of *Die Zauberflöte* sung by a young cast in the little baroque court theatre in the royal summer palace at Drottningholm, outside Stockholm. This lay forgotten like the castle of *Sleeping Beauty*, enveloped in dust and cobwebs until it was accidentally rediscovered in 1922 by an assistant from the Royal Library searching for a lost painting. In addition to the painting he found the original stage machinery installed in 1766 and 30 complete sets of scenery. The theatre is now in regular use for guest performances, many of which are directed by the English conductor Charles Farncombe.

USSR

Although opera might have been condemned as a decadent bourgeois entertainment, since the Revolution it has been officially encouraged and many new opera houses have been built in important centres, particularly since 1945. The two most famous remain the Bolshoi in Moscow and the Kirov in Leningrad. The Bolshoi is immense, and productions there tend to be extremely lavish and old-fashioned by Western standards. The Kirov, which dates from 1860, was the Maryinsky or Imperial Theatre until 1919 and received its present name in 1935 in tribute to the leader of the Leningrad Communist Party in the 1920s, Sergei Kirov.

Scene from Ingmar Bergman's film version of Mozart's opera The Magic Flute

Igor Stravinsky (1882–1971) never returned to communist Russia. A quarter of a century after *Oedipus Rex*, his opera/oratorio, was performed in Paris in 1927, he produced *The Rake's Progress* (Venice 1951), a true full-length opera with a libretto by W. H. Auden and Chester Kallman based on Hogarth's famous set of eighteenth-century pictures. Sergei Prokofiev (1891–1953), a pupil of Rimsky-Korsakov, also left Russia in 1918; his comic fantasy *The Love of Three Oranges* was premièred in Chicago in 1921, but *The Fiery Angel*, although written shortly afterwards and which he considered his finest work, was not performed until 1955 in Venice and has never received whole-hearted approval in Russia where he returned in 1934. His most ambitious opera was based on Tolstoy's epic novel *War and Peace* which he was still revising at the time of his death. It was finally performed in Florence in 1953 and in Leningrad in 1955.

Although composers, singers and musicians receive preferential treatment in the USSR, where they are acclaimed as 'people's artists', they have to toe the official line. Opera is considered a useful means of promulgating Soviet propaganda to the masses, but not only must the political message be acceptable, it's musical expression must also be beyond reproach. Anything unconventional or avant-garde tends to be condemned. Prokofiev was accused of *formalism*, that is, emphasising musical structure rather than the message the work was supposed to convey.

Dmitri Shostakovitch (1906–75) was criticised for *The Nose* (1930), based on a Gogol story, because it included 'eccentric effects of the onomatopoeic kind'! *Lady Macbeth of Mtensk* was at first acclaimed as a masterpiece, but two years later it was condemned in an article in the official newspaper *Pravda* under the heading 'Confusion instead of Music'. It returned to the Russian repertoire in 1963 in a revised version entitled *Katerina Ismailova*.

The most popular and uncontroversial Russian operas, apart from the classic repertoire of Tchaiskovsky, Glinka, Rimsky-Korsakov etc., are simple patriotic stories using lots of folk songs and colourful dances. Examples are *Daisi* (Twilight, 1923) by the Georgian composer Paliashvili and *The Quiet Don* (1935), based on Sholokhov's novel, by Dzerzhinsky (1909–78). Most of these works have not been heard in the Western world. Nor have the majority of fine singers which the country continues to produce. The greatest of them was Feodor Chaliapin (1873–1938). Born in

New Opera Company's production of The Nose *by Dmitri Shostakovitch (1973)*

extreme poverty in Kazan he excelled in all the leading bass roles but was unforgettable as Boris Godunov and Ivan the Terrible (Rimsky-Korsakov's *The Tsar's Bride*). Currently the best known Russian singers to Western audiences are the mezzos Irina Arkipova and Elena Obratsova, and the soprano Galina Vishnevskaya who, with her husband the 'cellist Mstislav Rostropovitch, left the USSR in 1974, and the bass Evgeny Nesterenko.

USA

The first reported opera performance in North America took place in Charleston, South Carolina in 1735, and was an English ballad opera, *Flora, or Hob in the Well*. The establishment of an international grand opera tradition goes back to 1825 and the season of Italian operas presented in New York by Lorenzo da Ponte (Mozart's librettist) and Manuel Garcia (father of two great prima donnas, Maria Malibran and Pauline Viardot-Garcia).

America became the land of golden opportunity for European singers and the sumptuous Metropolitan Opera House, which opened on Broadway and 39th Street in 1883, joined Covent Garden and Monte Carlo as one of the world's most prestigious and wealthy opera houses. It mounted celebrity seasons of incomparable splendour with casts of all the greatest singers of the day including Adelina Patti, Nellie Melba, Marcella Sembrich, two American sopranos who became established favourites in Europe, Emma Eames and Lilian Nordica, Jean and Edouard de Reszke, Feodor Chaliapin and the most popular of all, Enrico Caruso. Gustav Mahler and Arturo Toscanini headed the roster of conductors. From 1907 there was fierce competition between the 'Met' and Oscar Hammerstein I's Manhattan Opera House, but after three seasons Hammerstein was bought off and the general manager of the Met, Giulio Gatti-Casazza (who held the post from 1908 to 1935) was left unchallenged.

Italian by birth, Gatti-Casazza secured the world première of Giacomo Puccini's *La Fanciulla del West* (1910), appropriately set in a gold mining camp in California, followed by *Il Trittico* (Triple Bill), comprising *Suor Angelica*, *Gianni Schicchi* and *Il Tabarro* (The Cloak), in 1918.

The first opera by an American composer to receive its première at the Met was *The Pipe of Desire* (1910) by Frederick Shepherd Converse. One of the most interesting American operas introduced during this period was *The Emperor Jones* (1933) by Louis Gruenberg (1884–1964). A sad reflection of racial prejudice was that the obvious choice for the title role, the negro bass Paul Robeson (1898–1976), was disregarded in favour of the excellent white American baritone Lawrence Tibbett (1896–1960). Other American singers whom the Met nurtured for international stardom in the 1930s and 1940s included Grace Moore, Eleanor Steber, Astrid Varnay, Robert Merill, Jan Peerce, Richard Tucker and Leonard Warren.

Rudolph Bing, general manager from 1950 to 1970, was the first to engage negro singers: following Marian Anderson as Ulrica in Verdi's *Un Ballo in Maschera* in 1955, Gloria Davy became the first black Aida in 1958. Since then Leontyne Price, Grace Bumbry and Shirley Verrett have become some of the most sought after singers in the world. As well as his dispute with Maria Callas (1923–77) when she refused to alternate the roles of Lady Macbeth and Violetta in *La Traviata* in 1957, Bing will be remembered for accomplishing the transfer of the Met to its imposing new home at

New York's Metropolitan Opera House in the 1930s

the Lincoln Centre for Performing Arts. Flanked by the State Theatre, home of Balanchine's New York City Ballet and the New York City Opera, and the Philharmonic Hall, the five-arched facade shines out at night across the central piazza, its red and gold foyer dominated by two glowing murals by Marc Chagall.

The new house opened in 1966 with Samuel Barber's *Anthony and Cleopatra* but it did not meet with the same critical acclaim as his earlier opera *Vanessa* (1958) which has a libretto by Gian Carlo Menotti. Italian born Menotti, who writes the libretti for his own operas, has been the most successful of all American opera composers with *The Medium* (1946), *The Telephone* (1947), a short, comic curtain raiser, and *The Consul* (1950), all vital theatrical entertainments which have survived the gibes of cheap sensationalism. Elsewhere the search for successful American opera has foundered, although there have been works of interesting originality like Virgil Thomson's collaboration with Gertrude Stein, *Four Saints in Three Acts* (1934), George Antheil's *Transatlantic* (1930) which included hot jazz, and Marc Blitzstein's left-wing polemic *The Cradle Will Rock* (1937). The City Centre Opera (now New York City Opera and forging a new artistic policy under its general director Beverly Sills) mounted special seasons of American opera including Aaron Copeland's *The Tender Land* (1954), Carlyle Floyd's *Susannah* (1961) and Robert Ward's *The Crucible* (1961). George Gershwin's negro folk opera *Porgy and Bess* (1935) has as yet found no successors in popularity except in the field of the American musical. Stephen Sondheim's brilliant but commercially unsuccessful musical *Sweeney Todd* (1978) seems destined to find its place in the operatic repertoire, thus illustrating the indefinite distinction between the two genres.

Currently, no American city outside New York has a full opera season, although many centres either act as host to touring productions or import international celebrities for one or two specially mounted operas. The Boston (Grand) Opera Company flourished briefly after its foundation in 1908 and even toured Europe. In the 1940s Boris Goldowsky specialised in chamber

Gian Carlo Menotti's television opera Amahl and the Night Visitors *produced by the BBC in 1953*

opera with the New England Opera Theatre, and 20 years later Sarah Caldwell introduced an adventurous repertoire ranging from Schoenberg's *Moses and Aaron* (1968) to Roger Session's *Montezuma* (1976).

Chicago's Auditorium Theatre was opened in 1889 by Adelina Patti singing 'Home Sweet Home'. In 1910 it became home to the Chicago Grand Opera Company which enjoyed great success under the inspiration of soprano Mary Garden who had spent her childhood in Chicago. In 1921 Sergei Prokofiev conducted the première of *The Love of Three Oranges* which the company had commissioned. The Chicago Lyric Opera now give their performances in the Civic Opera House (1929) where Maria Callas made her American debut as Norma in 1954.

In San Francisco the Tivoli Opera House which provided grand opera in winter and light opera in summer was destroyed in the 1906 earthquake. The San Francisco Opera Company, founded in 1923 by Italian conductor Gaetano Merola, has been run for the past 30 years by Kurt Herbert Adler. It now ranks in repertoire and production standards as America's second company. Adler has also established Spring Opera as a show case for young singers, and Western Opera Theatre as a touring company for smaller towns on the Pacific coast.

One unique feature of American operatic life is the specialist departments of American universities which provide training and experience for young American singers, conductors, directors and designers, many of whom make their careers in European opera houses. Santa Barbara, California and Bloomington, Indiana have two of the best known opera departments.

5

Singing in opera

Because most people can sing naturally, providing pleasure for themselves if not for their listeners, it is sometimes difficult for the general public to appreciate the long years of intensive and specialised training that have to be undertaken by an opera singer. In general, actual voice training cannot start before physical maturity at the age of 16 or 17; before that age it is easier to assess a child's musicality and sense of pitch than how the singing voice will develop. As well as a good general academic education, children who may have a future as opera singers will best benefit from developing as general musicians and becoming proficient pianists so that they can accompany themselves and learn their own roles at the piano.

Boys in England have unrivalled opportunities for musical training in the cathedral choir system, auditioning at the age of eight or nine for a place in a choir school where they will take part in daily choral services, become proficient sight readers, develop their sense of rhythm and pitch and, particularly if they are of solo calibre, become oblivious to any fear of performing in public. Of course there is no guarantee that a boy soprano or alto will develop into an operatic tenor or bass. Many cathedral choristers go on to win choral scholarships to Oxford and Cambridge colleges which tend to produce intellectual singers more drawn to careers on the concert and oratorio circuit than to the more physical demands of the operatic repertoire. Robert Tear, Michael Rippon and David Wilson-Johnson are some of the British singers who have used this excellent early training as the basis for highly versatile and successful careers embracing opera.

A successful opera singer requires not only a good voice but intelligence, physical stamina, acting ability, an equable temperament and endless capacity for hard work. Most music colleges run their opera departments as post-graduate courses to which students come after a three-year course including piano or another instrument, a good basic musical training including harmony, music theory, history and languages, as well as having regular singing lessons. Only when they are vocally mature enough to sing operatic roles on stage at the age of about 21 are they eligible for opera departments like the Guildhall School of Music and Drama, the Royal College of Music, the Royal Academy or the Royal Northern College. Here they work with professional producers, conductors and music coaches, many of whom are on the staff of Covent Garden or the English National Opera; their studies will also include stage movement, mime, fencing, make-up, speech and drama. Sometimes students have a university degree in a completely different subject but have studied voice privately.

The first problem is how to start a career, particularly as very few singers are vocally mature before the age of 25; some join opera company choruses, hoping to be understudies and get small parts, and to survive the rigours of constant rehearsals and performances as one of a group rather than as an individual artist. Some win a travel bursary or scholarship for further study abroad. After working to pay for private singing lessons, I won an Austrian Government scholarship followed by an Arts Council grant for two years study at the Vienna Academy of Music and Dramatic Art where the opera course completes a seven-year study programme. The advantage of studying in Austria, Germany or Switzerland is that one learns the repertoire in German and is then prepared to audition for German opera houses. Düsseldorf, Cologne, Munich and Zürich all have opera studios which take a limited number of young singers each year with the idea of eventually using them within the parent company. Covent Garden has a similar scheme.

One of the dangers for a young singer is taking on roles which are too dramatic or 'heavy'; the main concern of opera companies is getting someone who can sing the part regardless of the long-term effects on that singer's career, and it is extremely difficult in an overcrowded profession for a singer to refuse an opportunity when it is offered. This is when the teacher or coach is able to advise which roles should be undertaken and how they should be tackled. The voice changes with physical and emotional maturity and this may require a change of singing technique; singers develop bad habits of which they themselves may be unaware and which need a 'third ear' to correct. Unlike an instrumentalist, the majority of singers continue to work with a voice teacher until well into their performing careers. Of course the relationship between teacher and established artist is very different from that between professor and immature student.

There is great mystique attached to the process of singing and waves of fashion as to which teachers are currently thought to be able to pass on the secrets of true *bel canto* singing or repair the ravages caused by vocal strain and previous faulty teaching. Singers are notoriously insecure and need a guru-like figure in the person of a teacher or reliable coach to whom they can turn for reassurance. Everyone flocks to the teacher of a successful singer hoping that the same sort of magic will be worked on them; with such an abundance of talent, a proportion of these new pupils will get to the top regardless of the teacher's methods, and his or her reputation will be enhanced despite the unfortunates who have their voices strained instead of trained and fall by the wayside.

There is no guarantee that the successful singer can pass on the secret of producing the marvellous sound, but sometimes the 'I do, you look and listen' method does work, particularly if the student has the same type of voice as the teacher. But the teacher who has worked out a successful method of teaching will be able to adapt it to a whole variety of voice types; the final element is the personal chemistry between teacher and singer and whether the emotional and psychological approach is the right one. Singing is essentially a physical activity and so the basis of good singing is correct breathing and abdominal support; only then can the larynx function correctly and all the resonators in the chest, pharynx and head be used. Teachers have a whole range of esoteric vocabulary and metaphors to try to explain the sensation the singer should feel when 'the sound is in the right place': 'think of a rugby football balancing in your throat', 'think of the sound supported by your breath like a ball at the top of a fountain', not to mention Peter Ustinov's teacher in Rome who wanted him to 'breathe with the forehead, think with the diaphragm and sing with the eyes' – all sound sense once one is attuned to the teacher's wavelength.

Like any other instrument, the voice has to be warmed up and most singers develop their own daily dozen of exercises, scales and arpegii, together with favourite phrases by which they can tell immediately whether everything is in order for the evening's performance. The average opera singer is a great, healthy extrovert who needs plenty of food, sleep and sex. Because their health is so important, singers tend to be hypochondriacs, avoiding extremes of heat and cold, both of atmosphere and of food and drink, and staying out of draughts and crowded, smoky places where they might pick up throat infections. In the case of a vocal emergency, the ear, nose and throat specialist is at hand. There are injections that can get a singer who is threatened by laryngitis through a performance, but the penalty is often paid afterwards, either by a loss of voice or by the weakening of the vocal chords taking its toll for a far longer period than if the one vital performance had been cancelled.

Emotional well-being is just as essential to a good performance as physical health and the strains of a marital break-up can wreak more havoc than bronchitis. Because the life of an opera singer is demanding, egocentric and of decidedly unsocial hours, the ideal partner is difficult to find. Young singers who marry fellow students sometimes find that the demands of their developing careers clash.

The length of a singer's professional life depends on many things including health, emotional stability, technique and luck. Lower voices take longer to reach full maturity and have a correspondingly longer life. Contraltos, whose roles are often witches, grandmothers and disappointed old maids, can grow comfortably old, fat and ugly, adding conviction to their parts, whereas sopranos are supposed to remain forever young and beautiful, except for the Marschallin in *Rosenkavalier* which is the ideal role for a woman who fears she is past her prime! Physical type usually goes with voice type, so that the majority of coloratura sopranos and soubrettes are small and pretty with lively temperaments and portray coquettes like Zerbinetta (Richard Strauss' *Ariadne*) or Despina (Mozart's *Cosi fan tutte*) with total conviction.

The most common female voice is the lyric soprano; Mimis for *La Bohème* are two a penny. The lucky ones develop more weight in the voice so that they can progress to heavy roles like Verdi's *Aida* or Wagner's Elsa (*Meistersinger*). Wagner presents the greatest challenge as his operas demand the heaviest and most dramatic voices; most baritones wait until their forties before attempting Wotan, and the heroic tenors and dramatic sopranos who can sustain a *Ring* cycle are very few. Lauritz Melchoir made the transition from baritone to *Heldentenor* (heroic tenor) thanks to the generosity of the English novelist Hugh Walpole who paid for him to take time off from operatic engagements and have the intensive lessons demanded by the change. Christa Ludwig, at the height of her mezzo career, became a dramatic soprano to sing Brünnhilde and Fidelio successfully but with nothing like the outstanding brilliance of her mezzo roles.

Nature sometimes fails to endow a singer with the physique to match the voice: the short weedy tenors who are no match for the six-foot sopranos but who long to sing the romantic leads instead of the buffo servants; the petite dramatic mezzos who are physically better suited to coloratura Rossini roles or travesti (boys) parts although the voice is that of an Amneris or an Eboli (Verdi's *Aida* and *Don Carlos*); the soprano who has the voice for *Salome* but whom no producer could ask to remove even the first of her seven veils!

In an overcrowded profession, excepting the obviously outstanding talents, success is very much a matter of luck as to whether a singer catches the ear of the right person at the right time. It is much easier to assess a singer in performance than in a ten-minute audition on a bare stage or in a rehearsal room with a piano. Agents act as talent scouts, signing up singers whom they then recommend for particular roles to conductors or producers casting specific productions, or to be put under contract to companies looking for particular voices for a variety of roles in the next season's repertoire.

Once a singer is with a company – the initial contract is usually for a year – life is dictated by their rehearsal and performance schedule and outside engagements can only be accepted with the permission of the management. Some idea of the roles to be sung will be given on signing the contract, but there will probably be some unpleasant surprises as the season progresses when details are finalised of the number of premières to be sung or whether the singer will be in the first or the second cast for a new production.

Certain productions may be retained by a company for many years: Covent Garden uses the outstanding Visconti version of

Luchino Visconti's production of Verdi's Don Carlos *at Covent Garden (1961)*

Verdi's *Don Carlos*, dating from 1958, and a house producer takes singers through the stage movements that Visconti originally planned. For a new production of an opera, the producer and the designer will meet many months in advance to discuss their visual and dramatic concept of the work so that the scenery can be built and costumes made. The conductor and the producer will decide the cast, and singers will usually have about two months of solo music rehearsals with a repetiteur at the piano to learn their roles. For a major Strauss role a singer may start work as much as a year before. There will also be sessions with a language coach for translation and pronunciation in singing.

Before stage rehearsals start, there will be a complete run-through of the opera at the piano with the conductor. Initial stage rehearsals of separate scenes will be in a rehearsal room with a piano and an assistant conductor, with the singers 'marking' their roles rather than singing full out. Most producers like to discuss the character and his or her motivation in depth with the artist before plotting the movements of a scene. The days are long since past when Madam Melba raised one arm to express emotion and both arms to express great emotion; although the voice is still of primary importance, dramatic plausibility is also required.

Meanwhile the conductor will be working with the orchestra and having separate rehearsals with the singers; all the forces meet for the *Sitzprobe* (seated rehearsal) which is a complete run through of the music without costumes or action. By this time the singers will have started to work on stage with the sets. The number of stage rehearsals with the orchestra depends on the complexity and familiarity of the work. Lighting plays a very important part in opera as it does in all stage productions, and the producer and lighting director will have worked closely with the rest of the technical staff before the final dress rehearsals in full costume and make-up. The customary final dress rehearsal before an invited audience gives performers a foretaste of public response, particularly useful for timing in a comedy, but no one can expect the same feeling at ten o'clock in the morning, with singers often saving their voices, as when the lights go down for the first night.

The presence of an audience always sets a singer's adrenalin flowing, but the knowledge that the impressarios, the press and other distinguished figures are all there making it a potential turning point in a career can inspire a singer to excel him- or herself. The ideal situation of at least two weeks of rehearsals in which all the cast can work together as a musical and dramatic ensemble is unfortunately rarely possible in international opera houses. Once a production has been launched, the cast may continually change and new artists will go on stage with just a *Verständigungsprobe* (explanatory rehearsal) in which they are taken through the basic moves without any time for the niceties of dramatic motivation. There is the practical problem of fitting costumes and wigs on artists of vastly differing sizes, hence some Carmens and Traviatas always travel with their own costumes regardless of how they match the rest of the designs. The most essential, old-fashioned opera prop is the prompter's box in the middle of the stage by the footlights, with that key figure mouthing the words to the singer just before he has to sing them.

Most roles will have a cover or understudy who must be available to go on stage at a few hours notice if the main singer is ill or injured. There is no more frightening feeling than going on stage with insufficient rehearsal, hoping not only to do one's self justice but that, like Birgit Nilsson, it may be the step out of the chorus to overnight stardom!

6

Going to the Opera

One of my pet theories is of the 'primitive' response to great art: there is only one occasion, the first time, that we experience Beethoven's Fifth Symphony or Shakespeare's *Hamlet* with no preconceived ideas (difficult in our culturally sophisticated society) and never again do we have the same opportunity of being completely and spontaneously overwhelmed. The loss of one's cultural virginity has compensations; not only does one know what to expect but one begins to compare performances. As one's response deepens from the emotional to the intellectual level, one begins to understand more of the artists' intention and see and hear below the surface of the work. The same process applies to opera.

An adolescent going to the opera for the first time, perhaps to Covent Garden or the Met for *The Tales of Hoffman*, will be impressed by the opulence of the surroundings, the glamour of the special occasion, the sense of excitement in the air, the magnificence of the costumes and scenery, the great waves of orchestral sound and the glorious melodies poured out by the singers. The intricacies of the plot and the incomprehensible language will not matter compared with the vivid impressions of romantic love, fairy tale mystery and evil magic.

Some people prefer to reserve their enjoyment of opera for the occasional special treat or expense account entertainment, a warm bath of sensuous pleasure. That pleasure can be enormously increased by a little intelligent homework beforehand. Frequent broadcasts of opera on radio and television, either as studio performances or relays from Covent Garden, the Met, Vienna or La Scala, bring the world's greatest singers on to the living room hearth rug. Public libraries make complete opera recordings available at very small expense, while the devotee can invest in expensive hi-fi equipment and build up a comprehensive collection of rare records so that he or she can compare great singers of the past with today's favourites. Because of the imperfections of early recording techniques it is difficult to judge the art of Patti or Melba compared with that of Callas and Sutherland, but it is possible to learn a great deal as to how tastes in voice and styles of singing have changed since the beginning of the century; today there is a preference for sopranos with a much rounder, warmer sound. The danger of recordings is that all the imperfections of a live performance are removed so that the listener becomes attuned to an artificially uniform standard of excellence which can never be achieved in the flesh.

Nevertheless, records are an excellent preparation for a live performance especially when combined with some background reading and a preliminary study of the story and a translation of the libretto so that one actually understands what is happening on stage. Invaluable standard reference books are Gustav Kobbé's *The Complete Opera Book*, Ernest Newman's *Opera Nights* and Harold Rosenthal and John Warrack's *Concise Oxford Dictionary of Opera*.

Learning to sing makes one appreciate that what is demanded from the operatic singer is far more complicated than singing in the bath! Amateur operatic societies still flourish, although the heyday of the drawing room tenor is long since past.

The amount of preparation that the opera goer is willing to undertake depends very much on how serious his interest becomes. One fascinating aspect of the birth of an opera is how the story is selected and converted from a novel or play into opera; reading Shakespeare's original version obviously adds an extra dimension to one's enjoyment of Verdi's operatic treatment of *Otello*. The correspondence between Richard Strauss and Hugo von Hofmannsthal discussing four of the six operas on which they collaborated gives a matchless insight into the way in which composer and librettist work together.

The relationship between words and music is a complex subject; why is it that certain literary masterpieces have been turned into great operas and others have perpetually eluded that transformation? The most obvious example is Verdi's success with *Otello* and *Falstaff* and Benjamin Britten's masterly version of *A Midsummer Night's Dream* contrasted with their mutual frustrated ambition to compose an operatic *King Lear*. Certain authors write works which are too full of characters and incidents to convert successfully into operatic terms, Dickens being the prime example, or their writing is too subtle or discursive, like that of Jane Austen or George Bernard Shaw.

Because action on the operatic stage is much slower than in spoken drama there are more opportunities for characters to reflect aloud or explore a situation in an introspective soliloquy. The orchestra can also recall past events and other characters by repeating key phrases from what has been heard before. A successful opera needs a clearly defined plot, strong characterisation and dramatic climaxes to exploit the whole range of emotional intensity which can be conveyed in singing far more effectively and powerfully than in normal speech. Where the words are already a perfect expression of drama and emotion, music has nothing more to add; very often it is the literary second rate which provides the operatic masterpiece, like *Carmen* from Prosper Merimée's novella, or *Tosca* from Sardou's 'sordid little shocker'.

Another of the librettist's considerations is the actual words the singer has to sing. The high notes that provide the climaxes of emotional intensity can not all be delivered on 'ah' sounds, the easiest sound to sing. English dipthongs and impure vowels create problems in singing not found with Italian. 'In unknown Tongues mysterious Dullness chant' was the eighteenth-century comment on Handel's Italian operas and the bulk of classical and romantic opera libretti are banal in the extreme, the arias and ensembles having endless repetition of the same phrases. This is at least more acceptable to the listener sung in a foreign language than translated into all too accessible everyday speech. W. S. Gilbert parodies the whole convention in *The Pirates of Penzance*: 'We go, we go' repeat the policemen ad infinitum, 'Yes, but you *don't* go' comment the girls.

With comedy, all the spice of the dialogue and humour of the situation is lost on an audience who do not understand the language fluently; there is a great art in translating the humour of one society and culture into that of another. Different languages have specific characteristics which lend a particular colour to the voice which can not be rendered in translation and account for the superlative voices which certain nations produce. *Boris Godunov* sung in English will sound completely different from the original Russian, as will *Carmen* sung in German or *Aida* in Czech. International opera singers have to be excellent linguists but provincial opera audiences are not; London, Vienna and Munich can provide the ideal solution by offering audiences a choice of opera in the original or in the vernacular, performed by two separate companies.

Many works which were considered impossibly avant-garde when they were first performed are now an accepted part of the repertoire; for example Alban Berg's *Wozzeck*, *Duke Bluebeard's Castle* by Béla Bartók and Stravinsky's *Oedipus Rex*, the Greek myth presented as a dramatic oratorio to a text by Jean Cocteau (Paris 1927). Arnold Schoenberg (1874–1951), the great pioneer of twelve-tone music or 'serialism' which has transformed composition during the last 60 years, never completed his biblical mystery play *Moses and Aaron*; it was performed after his death in Zurich in 1957, being enormously effective but extremely difficult to stage because of its musical demands on the chorus and orchestra.

The modernism of an opera depends on the treatment of its theme as well as its music. Luigi Dallapiccola (1904–75) succeeded with two issues of contemporary significance: the conflict between obedience to authority and individual desires in *Volo di Notte* (Night Flight, 1940), and the existence of individual freedom in a world of tyranny in *Il Prigioniero* (The Prisoner, 1950). These combined twelve-tone technique with Italian singability. Another Italian composer, Luigi Nono (b. 1924), made a strong criticism of contemporary society in *Intolleranza* (1960).

Because opera is the most expensive art form to produce and because the majority of opera-goers tend to be conservative in their tastes, preferring to hear what they already know and like, the public for contemporary and experimental works remains disappointingly small. The conventional opera house, with its orchestra pit and proscenium arch stage, is not conducive to experimental music theatre either. Nor are large luscious voices required for *Sprechgesang* (the cross between speech and song that Schoenberg first used in *Pierrot Lunaire*), short declamatory phrases and vocal lines of percussive repetition and enormous leaps. In fact today's composers, concerned with what the French composer and conductor Pierre Boulez has described as 'the unexploited worlds

Alan Berg's Lulu *with Karen Armstrong in a 1981 Covent Garden production*

in one's ear', consider that opera is an outdated and irrelevant musical form. Those who have written successful operas tend to be composers who are dismissed by the avant-garde as old-fashioned, like Britten, Henze, Menotti or Orff.

On the technical side, new developments in stage equipment, lighting and audio-visual effects have revolutionised opera staging. Pictures of past productions are a fascinating reflection of contemporary fashions in dress and decor which very often had nothing to do with the historical period in which an opera was supposed to be set. Today we expect far more historical accuracy, although the producer and designer may decide to shift an opera to another century because they prefer the costumes. The ultimate in *verismo* was the Zefirelli production of *Cav* and *Pag* at Covent Garden in which one could feel the heat of the sleazy Sicilian village and almost count the fleas!

Sometimes the setting can dominate the production, particularly if a distinguished and distinctive painter is called in as designer; this was the case with Salvador Dali's designs for *Salome* at Covent Garden in the 1950s which were artistically provocative but irrelevent to the subject matter. In 1981 David Hockney's striking backcloths and set designs provided an ideal Mediterranean background for a French triple bill of Satie, Poulenc and Ravel at the Met, and Sidney Nolan's painted gauzes for *Samson et Dalila* at Covent Garden gave it a feeling of primitive paganism which is all too often swamped in sentimentality. Changing moral standards now allow nudity on stage and scenes of far greater sexual explicitness than were envisaged by Saint-Saëns when he wrote *Samson et Dalila*. A modern-dress Carmen as a strip-tease artist and Escamillo as a racing driver can be very exciting but grand opera seems to work better if the orgies are confined to the chorus and the principals allowed to get on with the singing.

Opera can also be used didactically, presenting a political or philosophical theory. The 1981 production of *Fidelio* for the Welsh National Opera by Harry Kupfer from the Komische Oper is set in a concentration camp with a final tableau of freedom fighters surveying the coffins of Leonora and Florestan on stage. If *Figaro* is reinterpreted solely in terms of the class struggle, *Aida* is presented as being about black oppression, and *Traviata* is viewed as a tract against male chauvinism, all fashionably in keeping with current trends, the whole perspective of the works is distorted.

As far as experimental opera is concerned, the most interesting developments have been in the new range of sounds introduced by electronics and recording. One of the first works to combine these with conventional music was *Aniara* (Stockholm 1959), a space opera by Karl-Birger Blomdahl (1916–68). Others to exploit this potential were Johan Werle (b. 1926), another Swedish composer, with an opera in the round, *Dreaming about Thérése* (1965), and Luigi Nono with his opera *Intolleranza*.

Before the advent of television, radio presented opera composers with an attractive new medium in which the total effect is conveyed by sound. Werner Egk wrote his first opera *Der Zaubergeige* (The Magic Violin) for German radio in 1935; Boris Blacher (1903–75) made excellent use of radio's possibilities with *Die Flut* (The Flood, Radio Berlin 1946), a one-act chamber opera. Blacher and his Austrian friend and pupil Gottfried von Einem (b. 1918), whose operas have included adaptations of Büchner's *Danton's Death* (Salzburg 1947) and Kafka's *The Trial* (1953), both used distinctive musical personalities to produce modern works which were dramatically successful.

Film has proved a strangely disappointing medium for opera, though it is a useful way of presenting productions to a much wider public, as for example, Karajan's *Rosenkavalier* and *Carmen* and the Russian *Boris Godunov*. Because opera is slow moving, the camera has to find beautiful scenery to occupy the eye, hence the success of the Joseph Losey version of *Don Giovanni* which is set in Venice instead of Spain. The Michael Balcon *Tales of Hoffmann* conducted by Beecham made a great impression on me as a child, only equalled by *Carmen Jones* which was something totally new and different that could not be presented on an ordinary stage.

Television is now being used to relay international opera house productions round the world rather than for specially mounted studio performances or works commissioned for the medium such as Menotti's *Amahl and the Night Visitors*, *The Canterville Ghost* by the Swiss composer Heinrich Sütermeister (b. 1910), or Benjamin Britten's *Owen Wingrave* produced by the BBC in 1971.

The most exciting potential for the development of new operatic works and the reassessment of existing repertoire lies in 'total theatre', the term used by the French producer and choreographer Maurice Béjart for an art form involving singing, speaking, acting, dancing, painting, film ballet and tape montage.

Mozart's Don Giovanni *filmed by Joseph Losey with Ruggiero Raimondi as the* Don

Britain is still waiting to see the most successful German example of this, Zimmermann's *Die Soldaten*, which was premièred in Cologne in 1965. The British have to be content with experiments on a shoestring such as David Freeman's stimulating Opera Factory and Adam Pollock's Musica nel Chiostro. In the spring of 1981 I saw a realisation of Peri's *Euridice* performed in a disused film studio, with a modern reorchestration by Stephen Oliver, sung and acted around and inside a shallow circular pool of azure tinted water, which was totally spellbinding at 480 years remove from its creation in Florence in 1600.

Glossary

Alto

In Italian *alto* means 'high' and was originally used to describe the highest male voice. 'Male alto' is now used interchangeably with 'counter tenor' to describe a male voice which has broken but by use of exceptional head frequencies can sing a similar range of notes to the female contralto (G below middle C to E an octave and a third above it). The Germans divide female voices into only two categories and use 'alto' to cover mezzo-soprano and contralto.

Brindisi

A drinking song from the Italian 'to toast someone's health' used as a rousing aria usually with chorus joining in Italian opera. Verdi's *Macbeth* has a famous example.

Cabaletta

Final section of an aria with a strongly repeated rhythm, used most effectively to bring a long dramatic aria to an exciting finish.

Cadenza

An opportunity for a singer to display his technique in florid unaccompanied runs and leaps just before the end of an aria. These were originally improvised and left the orchestra and other singers hanging in the air, waiting for the final cadence.

Coloratura

From the Italian for 'colouring'; another term to describe vocal decorations and also for the type of high soprano required to sing with great agility above the stave in roles like The Queen of the Night (*The Magic Flute*) and Zerbinetta (*Ariadne auf Naxos*). The coloratura mezzo is a rare voice that can cope with specialised Rossini roles like Rosina and Cenerentola.

Competitions

One way in which young singers can be helped in their careers is by entering singing competitions which offer a scholarship for further training with a teacher or at an institution of the singer's choice, e.g. the Kathleen Ferrier or the Richard Tauber competitions. Alternatively, international competitions like Munich, Geneva, Toulouse or Rio de Janeiro may lead to a trial engagement in an opera house if the right people are on the Jury or in the audience.

Comprimario

Supporting singer specialising in small parts, often character roles like Spoletta in *Tosca* or Anina the intrigante in *Rozenkavalier*. Sometimes these parts are sung by beginners in an opera house in preparation for principal roles later.

Cover

An English term used as an alternative to 'understudy'. Sometimes a member of the company singing a small part or a chorus member is given a cover, i.e. asked to learn a main role and sit in on stage rehearsals so that he or she can perform the role in the event of the principal being indisposed.

Da capo

Italian 'from the beginning', a *da capo* aria is one in which the first section is repeated at the end giving the singer the opportunity to display his virtuosity by decorating the original tune with variations and ornaments.

Fach

The German word used to describe types of voice and the roles for which they are considered suitable, The *Spiel Altistin* is a contralto who will play character roles like Marcellina in *Figaro* or Suzuki in *Butterfly* but also Carmen and, depending on her age and the size of her hips, breeches roles like Cherubino (*Figaro*) and Niklaus (*Tales of Hoffmann*). The dramatic mezzo sings the Verdi and Wagner roles like Azucena (*Trovatore*), Amneris (*Aida*), Ortrud (*Lohengrin*) and Waltraute (*Götterdämmerung*).

Festivals

International opera festivals take many forms. The greatest Italian festival is held in the open in the Roman arena of Verona and mounts operas of unforgettable magnificence – real elephants in *Aida*. Bregenz (Austria) is an operetta festival mounted on a floating stage on Lake Constance. Some festivals are based on one composer: Spoletto was founded by Gian Carlo Menotti and Luciano Visconti; Montepulciano was founded by Hans Werner Henze and he used the town square for his stage in a highly effective reworking of *Don Chisciotte* by Paisiello in 1976. One of the most enterprising opera festivals is in Wexford in Ireland and is famous for reviving little-known masterpieces.

Maestro

Italian title of 'Master' given to the conductor or other distinguished musician. *Maestro di capella* was the term for the choirmaster of a court chapel; the German *Kapellmeister* is still the general word for conductor.

Mezza voce

Italian 'half voice', the composer's instruction for something to be sung quietly but without any lessening of expressive intensity.

Prima assoluta

First performance, usually referring to a world première.

Prima donna

First lady, used to refer to the leading soprano in an opera or an opera company, and also to the qualities that are commonly thought to be displayed by such ladies, namely egomania, temperamental outbursts when crossed, and demands for the entire world's constant love and attention.

Repetiteur

A French term in international use for the pianist who is responsible for rehearsing and 'repeating' a role with a singer until he knows it. An invaluable and long-suffering member of the opera house staff, it is often the first step for an aspiring conductor as he can learn the repertoire and conduct the off-stage band and chorus.

Soubrette

From the French meaning 'cunning' or 'sharp'; a light soprano, by definition young and pretty, who specialises in playing intriguing servant girls, both in opera and operetta, like Despina (*Cosi fan Tutte*) and Adèle (*Die Fledermaus*).

Spinto

Literally 'pushed on'; used to describe the type of voice which is a little heavier than a lyric but not as heavy as a dramatic, e.g. a *lyrico spinto* soprano is needed for Verdi's Desdemona, slightly heavier than Puccini's Mimi but not as heavy as his Tosca or Turandot.

Tessitura

The range of notes within which an aria or role is written and which determines whether it can be comfortably sung by a particular singer or not. It is not simply a question as to whether, for example, a tenor can sing a high C or not but whether the approach to the note makes it easy or difficult, and if phrases hover constantly round the highest limits of a voice they will be much more difficult to sing than the occasional thrilling high note as a climax.

Timbre

The French word for 'tone', it is used to describe the subtle differences between one voice and another. The basic difference between a bass and a baritone is not that the former has a better bottom to his voice and the latter a stronger top; it is the different colour and the darker, richer quality of the bass over the whole of the range compared with the more heroic ring of the baritone. In *Figaro* the music of all the female characters covers approximately the same vocal range but they are cast according to which voice suits the age and personality of the character: the lightest is Barbarina, a young immature girl, Susanna is a lyric soprano or soubrette, and the Countess is a more mature sounding soprano with a richer voice; Cherubino is a light mezzo in contrast with Marcellina who is an older mezzo but not a deep contralto because of the range and agility required. Similarly the master/servant relationship of the Count and Figaro is augmented by the darker voice used for the latter.

Workshop

Most American University music departments specialise in opera workshops where singers can rehearse and perform scenes from operas in informal dress with piano accompaniment and without elaborate scenery and stage setting. The idea is growing in England and can be a very useful way of introducing opera to new audiences, particularly school children. Opera North take excerpts performed in this informal way to local school halls and dining rooms and singers, conductor and producer explain to the children what opera is about and how a production is built up. Workshops on television in which famous singers work with young professionals on individual scenes also help to get to the heart of the music and the drama.

Bibliography

Brockway, W. and Weinstock, H. *The world of opera*, Methuen, London, 1963

Dent, E. J. *Opera*, Penguin, London, 1949

Grout, D. J. *A short history of opera*, 2nd edn, Columbia University Press New York, 1965

Hughes, S. *Great opera houses*, Weidenfeld and Nicolson, London, 1956

Jacobs, A. and Sadie, S. *Pan book of opera*, Pan, London, 1969

Kobbé, G. *The complete opera book*, edited and revised by The Earl Harewood, Putnam, London, 1976

Newman, E. *Opera nights*, Putnam, London, 1943
Wagner nights, Putnam, London, 1949
More opera nights, Putnam, London, 1954

Orrey, L. *A concise history of opera*, Thames and Hudson, London, 1970

Osborne, C. *The complete operas of Verdi*, Pan, London, 1969

Prawy, M. *The Vienna opera*, Weidenfeld and Nicolson, London, 1970

Rosenthal, H. *Two centuries of opera at Covent Garden*, Putnam, London, 1958

Rosenthal, H. and Warrack, J. *Concise Oxford dictionary of opera*, Oxford University Press, London, 1964

Westerman, G. von. *Opera guide*, Sphere, London, 1968

Index

Today opera is no longer the property of an upper-class intellectual elite. Television and radio have introduced its pleasures to a far wider audience. But there are still barriers to its enjoyment. The stylised singing, often in a foreign language, the seemingly obscure and convoluted plots, often following conventions established centuries ago, the rich and elaborate productions and the frequent breaks in the dramatic flow for long decorative arias – all conspire to leave the uninitiated bewildered and uncomprehending.

In OPERA, Carole Rosen, herself a professional singer of wide international experience, unravels the mysteries and describes the delights of this entertaining art-form. Beginning with its origins in religious dramas and its early development as a court entertainment, she traces opera's history through to the eighteenth and nineteenth centuries and the greatest practitioners of the art – Mozart, Verdi and Wagner. She describes how, as opera spread to all the great capitals of Europe, it was modified to suit each language and culture, and how the different operatic traditions became established. On the way, she gives an amusing account of the growth of light and comic opera.

Her stories give the reader a seat in the stalls at La Scala and the other great opera houses of the world and her anecdotes about the famous composers, conductors, producers, singers and impresarios take us backstage into the real world of opera.

The book ends with a chapter on the training and life of opera singers and a very helpful chapter on how to get